Pavilioned in Splendour

PAVILIONED
IN SPLENDOUR

A. A. THOMSON

Introduction by Tim Rice

THE PAVILION LIBRARY

First published in Great Britain in 1956

Text copyright © A. A. Thomson 1956
Introduction copyright © Tim Rice 1991

First published in the Pavilion Library in 1991 by
PAVILION BOOKS LIMITED
196 Shaftesbury Avenue
London WC2H 8JL

Series Editor: Steve Dobell

A CIP catalogue record for this book
is available from the British Library

ISBN 185145 6589

Printed and bound in Great Britain
by Biddles Limited, Guildford

INTRODUCTION

When it comes to conveying the character and appeal of the game and the sheer enjoyment to be had from it, there is scarcely a writer to match A. A. Thomson. It is tempting to say he must have been the most popular of all cricket writers, but probably that distinction belongs to Neville Cardus. Most people would concede that Cardus was the greatest – Thomson certainly believed that – and if by most popular we mean the most widely read, then Cardus was probably that too. I think one can say that Thomson was the warmest, the most romantic and very possibly the best-loved writer in the history of the game.

Unlike Cardus, Thomson wrote biographies, including one of W. G. Grace as well as his unusual and very successful 'double' lives, *Hirst and Rhodes* and *Hutton and Washbrook*. He also wrote a number of books on a single theme, such as *Cricket: the Great Captains, Odd Men In* and *Great Men of Kent,* but probably nothing suited him better than the wide-ranging, discursive form of his first three books. It is tempting to call them excursions, because they have something of the quality of a tour as he meanders, apparently spontaneously but with great artistry, through a kind of living museum of cricket. When, for example, he has clearly set off to get from A to B, one is soon conscious that in a series of graceful loops and detours he has taken in C, E and G and also paid his respects at D and F before nonchalantly ending his tour at H.

John Arlott put his finger on it, as so often, when he described A. A. Thomson as the happiest of cricket writers. He is the cricket appreciator *par excellence,* as indicated by the titles of his first two books on the game: *Cricket My Pleasure* and *Cricket My Happiness*. To prove (if proof were needed) that he is more than a lightweight popularizer, one only has to mention that the first book was enthusiastically introduced by Len Hutton *and* George Hirst, and the second by no less a figure than the magisterial C. B. Fry, who, after enlisting the help of Aristotle to define the difference between pleasure and happiness, defies us to find fault with the book. (With a champion like Fry, who needs introducing ever again?)

I have no doubt that Messrs Hutton, Hirst and Fry would have enjoyed Thomson's third book, *Pavilioned in Splendour*, just as much as the first two. Here he is again at his warm, chatty, rambling best. The book has a deep vein of nostalgia which, together with Thomson's own memories of the likes of Jessop, Hirst and Rhodes, gave him a special reverence for the Golden Age cricketers of his youth as well as the ability to write about them from first-hand experience. Not that he is ever a bore about the good old days. He writes with equal enthusiasm about Hobbs and Hammond, Hutton and Compton, as well as the new star, Peter May, and it is clear that for Thomson all ages have had their seams of gold.

Nor is it only the spectacular players whom he celebrates. In a chapter entitled 'Some Uncles and Nephews', in which he toys with the idea of reincarnation in cricket, he suggests that there is a link between K. L. Hutchings and the young Colin Cowdrey, two cricketing cavaliers, but is no less taken with the idea that Trevor Bailey, so often England's stubborn sheet anchor in the Fifties, could be related in some way to the equally limpet-like J. W. H. T. Douglas. Indeed, whether he is writing about victorious English tourists in Australia, outstanding captains, great South African players or the Yorkshire sides he watched at Lord's and the Oval from the Edwardian era to the 1950s, it is character in action, as much as prowess, that appeals to Thomson's imagination. Doubtless, had he lived through the 1970s he would have found the mature Geoffrey Boycott as fascinating to watch and write about as the more obviously talented and entertaining Richards boys, Barry and Viv. How well he would have brought out the contrast in style, approach and temperament between David Gower and Graham Gooch!

Inseparable from character in cricket is humour, and there is a strong current of it running through this book. 'You've got him in two minds,' says the fielder helpfully to the bowler, '...he doesn't know whether to hit you for four or six!' Every village trundler has had to put up with this gibe from time to time, and for the non-bowler I am told it remains exquisitely funny, but how many realize that it is over fifty years old? From Thomson we learn that the batsman who occasioned the remark was the South African H. B. Cameron, and that it was delivered by Arthur Wood to, of all bowlers, Hedley Verity! Beleaguered bowlers need not feel quite so bad in future when subjected to this sally. Thomson has a tremendous repertoire of cricketing anecdotes and one-liners (many of them apocryphal no doubt – but who cares?), which he weaves into his narrative with consummate skill and retells with the verve of a professional comedian.

My only reservation about A. A. Thomson when I used to read his books in the 1960s was that he was very clearly a Yorkshireman. (He wasn't actually – he was a Scot, but he adopted Yorkshire at a very early age.) This was not entirely his fault, I admit, but at the end of the Fifties and for most of the Sixties I and a few million other cricket-lovers had a bit of a problem with Yorkshire. They won the championship seven times in ten years and had a habit of inflicting humiliating defeats on other counties and causing much unhappiness to the impressionable young cricket nut. In short – and this may sound a bit funny in 1991 – they were a bit too good.

However, while Yorkshire may have been insufferable, Thomson's allegiance to the white rose was not. He had clearly suffered himself. Before Yorkshire's reign of terror began, after all, Surrey had won the championship seven times in succession. Yes, Thomson understood.

Another fine writer (and another Yorkshire partisan, as it happens), Alan Gibson, once wrote that he never much enjoyed watching Hutton, his hero, bat. 'I was always scared that he might get out, like a housewife who is so proud of the best china that she never takes it out of the cabinet.'

In *Pavilioned in Splendour*, while recalling Yorkshire–Middlesex games at Lord's, Thomson speaks for all helpless partisans when he writes:

> The 1955 match was an interesting example of a theory of mine. Your ideal spectator always has two notions

in his mind: he wants to see his own side win and he wants to see the game played as excellently as it can be played. There are some who claim that they do not care who wins so long as it is a good game. It may be so...To be without prejudice is an admirable attitude, no doubt, but somehow it is possible to suspect its sincerity. If I were watching a match played between penguins of the north pole and penguins of the south pole, I should shout like mad for the north, if only to warm the game up a bit. The man that hath no partisanship in his soul is fit for treasons, stratagems and spoils: let no such man be trusted. Having said that, I readily agree that the other thing is important, too.

I particularly like the last sentence. He seems to be admitting that in an ideal world we would all be objective, not partisan; but so perfunctory is this guilty-sounding after-thought that the clear implication is that in an ideal world, well, we wouldn't be human, would we?

Thomson himself could hardly be more human. A few hours in his company at a Yorkshire game, I suspect, would have had even the most resentful southerner cheering for his beloved county. As John Arlott once wrote: 'Mr Thomson writes with a nostalgia, a wealth of anecdote, a warmth and heroic strain which, if we were not careful, would make Yorkshiremen of us all.'

TIM RICE
LONDON 1991

PAVILIONED
IN
SPLENDOUR

by

A. A. THOMSON

To
NEVILLE CARDUS
who, as surely as W. G. GRACE was
THE GREAT CRICKETER,
is
THE GREAT CRICKET WRITER

Contents

CHAPTER 1

THE TWO ARCHBISHOPS

I

IT IS an old story of mine that the line from the hymn,
'Pavilioned in splendour,' once filled me with visions of some
vast empyrean amphitheatre encircling a sea, not of crystal,
but of emerald; of a heavenly pavilion, shaped not like those of
Lord's or the Oval, but like the pavilions in the *Idylls of the
King*, gleaming, mystic, wonderful; and of a reverend figure,
looking a little like Lord Hawke, golden coronet and all, for
ever gazing down from his throne in some celestial Long Room.
I have visited many terrestrial pavilions since then and,
frankly, they do not strictly resemble the silken tabernacles
of my dreams. But the tradition, the air, the mysterious
sense of the past is unchanged. The glory has not wholly
departed.

It is the same with players as with pavilions. The cricketers
whom I know today are normal, pleasant, intelligent, highly
skilled people, but they are creatures by no means too good for
human nature's daily food. The cricketers of half a century ago
were different. To us boys they were heroes, paladins, romantic
as the knights of King Arthur's Round Table. Their arms we
knew : their greaves, their gauntlets, their brands Excalibur.
Their features for the most part were weather-beaten and
homely, for seldom did we see so tremendously handsome a
fellow as C. B. Fry, and when we did, the deadliness of our
hostility towards this high-ranking enemy obscured our judgment.

Oddly, this childish fancy was not in essence absurd; it was
even righter than we knew, for if ever there was an ideal
knight, at least in Tennyson's Arthur's fashion, it was a man
like George Hirst, immensely strong but gentle, steadfast, un-
daunted, and above all shiningly chivalrous. This was true,
whatever else was fancy.

9

Apart from the hymn and the comparison of our heroes with Arthur's knights, we had a slight tendency to drag theology in. At eight or nine I took, owing to my Scottish background, a much sterner view of church organisation than I should feel free to maintain now. The form I then favoured was a Presbyterianism of the grimmer kind. I did not know that Charles II had described this form as no religion for a gentleman, and if I had known I should not have cared. I disapproved of the man. Life was too real, too earnest for Merry Monarchs.

My particular friend, whose father was a clergyman, favoured the episcopal errors of the Church of England bishops. I was against bishops. I scorned my friend's bishops and challenged him to produce his authority for their existence, or at least to tell me who they were. He did not know their names but he offered me two archbishops. And who were they? The archbishops of Canterbury and York. Yes, but who *were* they? Who was the Archbishop of York for instance? He should, as a sign of faith, at least tell me that. My friend faltered, swallowed and said:

' Lord Hawke.'

' And who is the Archbishop of Canterbury?'

' Why, Lord Harris, of course.'

I accepted his assertion and, although this was the period of philosophic and religious doubt, did not conceive the slightest doubt on the subject until some considerable time afterwards. The more I consider the matter, the more I feel it is a pity that my friend's statement contained errors of fact. Speaking without the least disrespect for the contemporary holders of those high offices, I feel that Lord Hawke and Lord Harris might have ruled their provinces with high distinction. They were men of integrity and authority, men who nothing common did or mean, men who would have given their lives for the faith that was in them. And, following their strongest characteristic, they would have stood no dam' nonsense from anybody. On the whole, with the deepest respect, it seems a great pity . . .

II

When Lord Hawke, as the Hon. M. B. Hawke, took over the captaincy of the Yorkshire eleven in 1883, he was a Cambridge undergraduate and he entered on his task both as a labour of love and as a kind of Christian duty. The captaincy of Yorkshire in the eighties was no sinecure. The side was like a cheerful, delightful, skipperless pirate crew, whose mates had stood watch turn and turn about, pretty much as they felt like it. When Lord Hawke first mounted the bridge, they were eleven highly talented rumbustious individualists, but hardly a team. When he retired in 1910 he left behind him a powerful phalanx, a disciplined band of brothers. The team he captained at the beginning of the century was potently armed at all points and was, in fact, almost certainly the most formidable county eleven that ever walked on to a field.

Steadily he reduced his magnificent but motley robber-band to shape and order and, though he was the kindest of men, this could not all be done by kindness. He was strict. He had to be. And, in a county where a diamond is hardly considered a diamond unless it is rough, there was a good deal of polishing to do. Some players continued to be difficult for some time, but from the earliest days there were those who gave willing service and there was never a captain who had more loyal lieutenants. These were George Ulyett and afterwards John Tunnicliffe and, above all, George Hirst. Yorkshire's cricketers had not merely to play well but to behave well and they were expected to pay as much attention to their personal appearance as though they had been recruits to the Brigade of Guards. Lord Hawke's great ancestor was the sailor hero of the battle of Quiberon Bay and maybe there was a touch of naval discipline in his county leadership. If so his players reacted with that pride and loyalty which the Royal Navy somehow above all other services evokes.

As a cricketer, Lord Hawke was a far more talented performer than, at this distance of time, he is given credit for. In his career he made over 13,000 runs and thirteen centuries. He was a fine fielder, a fine strategist and a hard hitter at No. 7 or No. 8, who could be stubborn or violent as the state of the game demanded. One of his most attractive innings lies embedded in the score-sheet of the 1896 Yorkshire v. Warwickshire match at Edgbaston. In that mastodon-like total of 887, still the highest of county scores, he made 166 and, with Peel, put on a colossal addition of just under 300 runs for the eighth wicket. In those classic elevens at the turn

of the century Yorkshire's amateur captain was first-class but
not a passenger.

In his early days he travelled the world with the fervour
of a missionary and there were few corners of the globe in
which he did not attempt to play, whether the pitch was of
turf, matting or mud. He visited Australia in 1887-88 in one
of the two sides which so surprisingly toured the Antipodes
in that season. (One is reminded of the line in A. A. Milne's
delightful play, *Belinda*: 'Dear me, how simultaneous of
them!') Later he shepherded teams twice through America
and Canada and South Africa and once through India, New
Zealand and South America. Of all these touring sides he
was, in addition to his other manifold qualities, a distinctly
valuable playing member.

I have said that to us small boys he represented ultimate
majesty. Our elders, of all ranks, regarded him with the
profoundest respect. Even from the rough and ready demo-
cracy of the West Riding he received his due. It is only a
man of the highest quality who can gain and keep the reverence of the naturally irreverent.

I have sometimes found people of a later generation whose
ideas on Lord Hawke were vague but derogatory. (Wasn't
he the chap who had words with his Maker about the horrors
of professional captaincy?) Now Chesterton once said that he
never minded people calling him a thin, teetotal Protestant,
because it was demonstrably untrue. Similarly, if there was
one man who, more than any other in cricket history, showed
himself a true friend to professional cricketers, it was Lord
Hawke. More than his twenty-seven years of captaincy, his
twenty-eight years as county president, his prowess as a
player, his work as a selector and his wisdom as an elder
statesman—more than all these things stands out his untiring and unselfish work to improve the status and rewards
of the professional. He made it his business to see that the
hitherto ill-paid pro. had a living wage, that he should gain
regular (and regularised) talent money for a good performance, that he should receive the unheard-of benefit of winter
pay, that his official benefit should be properly planned and
executed and, perhaps most important of all, that a proportion of his benefit money should be securely invested for him.
All these blessings Lord Hawke procured for the Yorkshire

professional; what Yorkshire had done Kent were quick to follow, and if Yorkshire and Kent made such improvements, could other counties be far behind? Thus so far from being the foe of the pro., he was the benefactor of every professional in the land, of his own time and since.

His too-often quoted observation on professional captaincy has been subjected to virtually the worst distortion in history since Bismarck altered the Ems telegram.

I approach the subject of what a good man may have meant in a particular utterance with a diffidence rarely found in critics who tell us what Shakespeare meant and divines who go even further, but it is my humble belief that Lord Hawke was not flinching from a time when a professional would be England's captain, but from a time when there would be no more amateurs good enough to be captain of the side or even to find a place in it. He hated the idea of a game, unbrightened by the best type of amateur like, say, K. L. Hutchings. So do I. If we are lucky enough to have young men like May and Cowdrey, let us cherish them, for they are precious as rubies. The best captain is the best captain, be he short or tall, north or south, amateur or professional. I would suggest that Hutton in captaincy showed very much the same qualities as Lord Hawke himself showed—resolution, sound strategy, and a determination to get the best out of men and conditions. There could have been nothing but mutual respect between those two strong personalities.

Lord Hawke was imperfect, even as we are imperfect. He could take an imperious and sometimes narrow view and he had, like many more between Tees and Humber, a habit of regarding Yorkshire as more important than the rest of the universe. Nevertheless, nobody in the great days doubted his stature. If in those years you had gone into a pub and seen any of the old professionals drinking his glass of ale, and if you had ventured to say a word against his Lordship, you would have started something. That professional—whether it was Ulyett, Tunnicliffe, Hirst or any of half a dozen others —would simply have knocked you down. He would, I say, though a modest, peaceable, amiable, good-humoured, tolerant soul, have knocked you down. And it would have served you right.

III

Lord Harris gave to cricket the same sort of unselfish service as his forebears of several generations had given to civil and military administration in India. He came from a family set in authority and he wore the purple naturally. In the Eton eleven of 1868 he had as his companions C. J. Ottaway, one of the heroes of Cobden's match two years later, and C. I. Thornton, the man who put Scarborough Festival on the map and by his gigantic hitting nearly knocked it off again. Harris did not go up to Oxford in time for Cobden's match. This was his last year at school and under his captaincy Eton, in a more exciting match than usual, beat Harrow by 21 runs. At Eton they were instructed by R. A. H. Mitchell, who was reckoned the most stylish bat and most skilful coach of his day. In Harris's cricket at the university he did little of note until his third year, when his 43 on an atrocious pitch helped to bring victory to Oxford.

His playing connection with Kent was even longer than Lord Hawke's with Yorkshire. His attitude towards his beloved county was exactly the same as his friend's : that of a wise and benevolent guardian who could be stern when occasion demanded. His first game for Kent was in 1870 and his last was in 1911, when he turned out against an All-Indian eleven at the age of 60 and made 36 in his only innings. He also bowled ten overs, taking one wicket for 34. One had imagined that only W.G. himself would have so defied the years, but Harris actually played for the M.C.C. as late as 1919, if not later. If a man will play when approaching seventy, there is no reason why he should ever give up and I toy with the fancy that somewhere in a Kentish field, that wonderful old gentleman may still be playing . . . Perhaps 1906 was the happiest year of his life for that year Kent won the county championship and everything in the garden of England was lovely.

In between those two extreme dates he captained Kent from 1875 to 1889 and these were years for Kent of cricket ripe as its own cherries and sunny as Festival days at Canterbury. Besides playing for Kent, Lord Harris loved to turn out for Eton Ramblers, I Zingari, who were the only begetters of Canterbury week, and the Band of Brothers, better known as the B.B. The club was founded by some exuberant young officers of the East Kent Yeomanry who invented for themselves a uniform consisting of a red shirt, white knicker-bockers and a big sombrero, but later they took life more decorously and in time became the nursery for Kent amateurs.

His tours abroad were many and varied. While still at Oxford he went to Canada and the U.S.A. on that pioneering expedition rather boisterously described by R. A. Fitzgerald in *Wickets in the West*. This was the tour on which W.G. made his famous one-sentence speeches. W.G. said that he and Lord Harris had only two things in common: they were both bad sailors and bad speakers, which was a little hard on his lordship. In 1878-79 Harris took a side to Australia. Only one Test was played and easily won by Australia, mainly because, while Tom Emmett, though 'hard as a board and active as a cat', could not bowl at both ends, Spofforth (six for 48 and seven for 62) apparently could. On this tour, in the match with New South Wales, an angry mob of Sydney larrikins invaded the pitch with a view to lynching one of the umpires, who had been so misguided as to be born in Mel-bourne. They met with a surprising reception. 'Monkey' Hornby carried off its ring-leader bodily into police custody, George Ulyett distributed the six stumps as defensive weapons, and Lord Harris observed calmly, as though settling some petty nursery dispute. 'No, no, George, we must do nothing wrong.'

Harris captained his country in three Tests in England: once in the first Test ever played in England (1880) and twice in 1884. That first Test was the only one in which the three Graces appeared for England together. W.G. compiled England's first Test hundred, and made it a glorious hun-dred and fifty for good measure. E.M. made 36 and a duck, and Fred bagged a brace, but made the most talked-of catch of the century, taking Bonnor off a colossal ballooning hit which stayed up in the upper atmospheric envelope while two runs had been made and a third started. England's captain made a stylish half-century and England won by five wickets.

Lord Harris permitted political ambition to interrupt his cricket career. 'It is,' said W.G., 'the only bad thing I know about Lord Harris.' His political career was distinguished, both in India where he pioneered and fostered cricket, especially among the Parsees, and at home when for a comparatively short time he was Under-Secretary for India under Lord Randolph Churchill. After giving up parliamentary office—he was probably far too independent of mind for what is now called the party line—he went into the City.

One of the cricketing campaigns associated with his name is the war—he called it a ' desperate fight '—against what he considered unfair bowling. This was always a controversial subject and he did not mind controversy in the least. Lancashire possessed at least two bowlers who, in his opinion, frankly threw. So high did feeling rise in these matters that Kent cancelled matches with Lancashire, because of the questionable action of Crossland (very fast), and Nash (slow). The following year these two bowlers did not appear in the Lancashire side and fixtures with Kent were resumed. Lord Harris claimed that public opinion had ' killed the evil,' but he himself had roused the opinion.

He was, like his fellow-peer, imperious and, in controversy, even fiery. Such was his commanding force of character that cricketers, young and old, stood in awe of him. Yet no one could say that he ever had anything but the good of the game at heart. If cricket, in his own words, was and is ' more free from anything sordid, anything dishonourable, any savouring of servitude than any game in the world,' then for this freedom cricket owes as much to him as to any man. The phrases that enshrine his most cherished feelings are part of the classic literature of the game :

' To play it keenly, honourably, generously, self-sacrificingly, is a moral lesson in itself and the classroom is God's air and sunshine. Foster it, my brothers . . . protect it from anything that would sully it, so that it may grow in favour with all men.'

SOME YORKSHIREMEN AT LORD'S

CHAPTER 2

I

IF WINTER comes, can spring be far behind? The answer is in the affirmative. Spring can be a long way behind. But winter ends at last and even while milk comes frozen home in pail there is a chance that something may be happening in a hemisphere more sensibly situated than ours. In some corner of a foreign field an M.C.C. touring side may even have won a rubber. The thought is good for the chilblains. Almost better, if anything can be, than the knowledge of touring triumphs far afield is the thought that cricket is beginning again in English fields, from the stately homes of Lord's and Headingley to the bumpy meadows of the countryside which have a swathe twenty-two yards long and, alas, not very broad, cut out of the middle. There may be a chestnut tree at short-leg and a slit-trench at deep third man, but it is for ever England.

Springtime, if and when you get it, is a good thing in its own right. There are few sights more pleasing than that of the first crocuses and early daffodils and there is something heart-warming in our annual relief on learning that chill winter has not done them in and that the local authorities have not taken them away from us for some high-sounding but essentially evil purpose.

But for me the supreme moment in all the glad New Year is the moment when I pass through the turnstiles at Lord's at the opening of the season.

I generally, like other wise men, approach from the east, but it does not matter. Heaven has many gates. Having paid your two shillings (and better value for even a north-country-man's money it would be hard to find) you pass through the broad canyon between the high south wall and the Mound stand; quickening your pace, you swing round to the right by the bookstall and the full glory of the picture bursts upon you.

With a lover and his lass, the reality, when he sees her once more, is even more beautiful than the image he has been carrying in his heart. So it is with Lord's. All through the winter, while the north-east wind howls round the eaves and the snow lies thick on the garden borders, you have comforted yourself with your imagined picture of this last Saturday in April. Now it breaks upon you if more grandly than you imagined. To your left is the great terra-cotta bulk of the most renowned pavilion in the world; and it is a solemn thought that the original building had a thatched roof; to the right, beyond the Mound, the widely curved high bank of the open stands, with the sight-screen before and the Nursery behind. (It once really was a market garden nursery.) The sight-screen for most of its life had been painted in a very slight variant of the ancient dead-white; now it is a delicate shade of blue, reminiscent of a sea-gull's egg. Right in front of you across the green width of the playing area is the Father Time stand, with the main scoreboard, virginally blank, in the middle, and the old gentleman himself on top.

You set out on your first walk round the estate (which is a kind of sacred pilgrimage); past the Tavern, under whose veranda you see a gentleman, probably a well-known actor, appreciatively holding up a glass of golden ale to the light; past the clock tower; the Q (members and friends) stand; the closed court behind the pavilion where the first schoolboys linger with their autograph albums, hopeful and eager as the first snowdrops, waiting for a glimpse of one of the earth's great ones.

By the time you have made the circuit of the other half of the great round-edged rectangle past the Father Time tea-bar and round by the opening where lie the covers which you hope will never be required, you hear the sound of music which affects you as the skirl of the pibroch affects a Scot or the fire-iron infelicities of a contemporary symphony affect those who take their pleasures in that sad way. It is the sound of the pavilion bell, playing a carillon unique in music: delightful though dignified, solemn but genial. You hurry round to stake your claim to a place on the wooden seats in front of the Tavern. The seats are hard, and you can soften

them for sixpence, but if you are a hardy northerner, you
scorn soft seats. You look round. The crowd is not very large
—it will be considerably bigger after lunch—but it is composed of lovers of the game, people who, like yourself, want
at the moment nothing so much in life as to see another
season launched upon its happy voyage. It would be well
worth cracking a bottle of champagne over. Before you
stretches the magic expanse of emerald green that has seen
struggle and drama, character and comedy, on good wickets
and bad, for nearly a hundred and seventy years. In the
nearest corner the Lord's sparrows flit and twitter, as they
or their ancestors have undoubtedly flitted and twittered for
the same hundred and seventy years.

The bell tolls again. Then with that measured tread which
is the acme of official dignity the umpires come down the
steps and out through the wicket gate. Their long white coats
have something of the reverend quality of ecclesiastical vest-
ments. You inevitably contrast them with the truncated gar-
ments of the Australian umpires, who, in the newsreels at
least, are hardly distiuguishable from grocers or even den-
tists. Compare the English and Australian umpire, each in
his characteristic costume : one is a bishop, the other might
well be a barber. It is perhaps fortunate that it is not really
a small world.

Our two bishops reach their appointed stations. Figures
in white flannels are moving in the pavilion's main doorway.
Then you settle down to perfect happiness because the first
match of the season has for a long time been M.C.C. v.
Yorkshire. If Yorkshire field first, well, there you are; you
will see them troop out all at once, familiar figures under the
white rose cap, with perhaps one or two unfamilar ones, too.
And if Yorkshire are having first turn at the wicket, you may
see the finest batsman in the world.* The bell, the umpires,
the fielding side and at last the two batsmen. Blossom by
blossom the spring begins . . .

II

But Lord's is not the only place in the United Kingdom

---

* Alas, you will see Hutton no more at the wicket, but you may settle
comfortably for Lowson, Wilson, Watson and one or two others.

where the hounds of spring are on winter's traces. In every club, old or new, majestic or lowly, preparations follow their appointed and hallowed way. In my old Essex village of Steeple Thatchby we would go up to the field beyond the friendly local railway which has now been abolished by Act of Parliament and every evening of the week before our first game we would solemnly carry out the ritual of practice. We would erect our net, which was far more reticulated than any other net you ever saw, against the hawthorn hedge in the corner and every member who looked likely to pay his subscription later would have five minutes' batting to as many bowlers as could find crickets balls in the old club bag. As long as a large enough number of balls remained to fulfil their destiny by being knocked over the hedges, we were content to go on knocking, because cricket balls were not then so sinfully costly as they are today. Even so, there would come a moment when the honorary secretary, a patient, thoughtful and mildly pessimistic character, would judge that the supply of ammunition was running short, and protest: ' Look, chaps, we positively must keep one ball for Saturday's game. Besides, there's the pitch . . .'

Thereupon we set about the reclamation of the central rectangle of turf which Farmer Pimstrim allowed us for our fun. After we had removed the posts and wire, set up to thwart the curiosity of our landlord's shorthorns, old Joe Bush, our star performer with the scythe, would set to work. Joe with a scythe was a more entertaining performer than most cricketers with a bat. His style, if one must suggest a comparison, was in the vein of Eric Hollies rather than that of Peter May. His late-cuts were terrific. Nobody could ever have called Joe a smooth operator, but, when he had finished, at least the first hay-crop of the season had been removed. Our next step was to put on the heavy mower. No, not the heavy roller. Most clubs possess a heavy roller, but we had a heavy mower. It could not be said that one man went to mow, because ours was an ancient juggernaut of immense weight with blades as awe-inspiring as those attached to the wheels of Boadicea's chariot. Whenever we used it, six men went to mow : two to pull, two to push, and two to say : ' Whoa, there, steady . . .'

When we had finished, the pitch was perfect. At least it was perfect for a bowler of the apparent amiability of Wardle or Titmus to bowl on. But if it were bowled on by bowlers of the velocity of Tyson, Statham or Trueman, the result would vary violently between mayhem and manslaughter. Yet somehow we survived to tell the tale and this was mainly due to our courage, our endurance and the fact that the most hideous of the bumpers went sailing at incredible altitudes over the wicket-keeper's head. Nevertheless we managed to get our season under way somehow. And if old Joe marked our whitewashed crease in freehand style without the aid of a guiding board, he had the satisfaction of reflecting that Leonardo da Vinci would probably have done it in the same way. The happy thought was, is, and ever will be, that cricket started, starts and will go on starting at the beginning of May as long as England, that odd but likeable country, shall endure.

III

The first game of the season, as we have seen, is M.C.C. against Yorkshire and this should be a cheerful affair, even if the weather is coldish, the sky is darkish and the fielders wear so many sweaters that they lack only goldfish bowls over the top of their heads to look like taxi-men flying through space. The next game that especially interests Yorkshire exiles is the Middlesex match, which takes place in July. By that time summer is truly in and you will see Lord's at its most welcoming. Unless it is raining. Then you will see the Tavern at its most welcoming. Life at its worst has certain compensations.

I am thinking of the last two Middlesex v. Yorkshire matches I have seen. Normally, you will understand, I see only one day of a three-day match and it is a matter of sheer chance whether my day is the day of the match or not. Some men are fortunate enough to watch every day of every important game free and, what is more, receive money for accepting the privilege. It is a sad thought that some of them do not appreciate this as a high honour and only do it for the money. This attitude can become an occupational disease of critics. There are brilliant and indeed noble exceptions, but frequently theatre critics come to hate the theatre, film critics to detest films and people who are paid to watch games develop a sad sort of sophistication, not to mention acidity of the stomach. And that is why I have never been to a first-class cricket match without paying at the gate. As we say in the north, it keeps you independent-like.

The first day of the 1954 Middlesex v. Yorkshire game saw some grand batting. I had always admired Willie Watson; his batting, like the man himself, is of 24-carat quality. I had not realised before how attractive a player was Vic Wilson, that burly young farmer from the Malton district, who hit the ball that day about as hard as a ball could be hit and still remain ball-shaped. The contrast in style between the two left-handers was instructive and fascinating, especially in their off-side strokes. Here was Watson, all trim elegance, playing the classic cuts and drives with charm and delicacy; and there was Wilson, hammering 'em like a Clydeside ship-yard worker, as if he meant the ball to stay riveted to the boundary rails. The muscles of those powerful forearms were strong as iron bands. It may be that it was this innings which helped to win him a place in Hutton's 1954-55 touring side in Australia, and it is a pity that, for one reason or another (but most for lack of practice), he did not have a successful tour with the bat. He made up for this deficiency, however, by turning out frequently as twelfth man in the big matches and being the best fieldsman in sight.

The most difficult thing for a Yorkshireman about that game at Lord's was that though Yorkshire, thanks to Wilson and Watson, made a big score, Middlesex made a bigger. For this success they were indebted to Robertson, who made a copybook century, and to a dark-haired youngster named Don Bennett, who batted as confidently as a man who had been playing cricket for years and compiled the highest score of his young life. There were times when his style looked like a reflection, not pale and by no means unconscious, of the great Denis Compton's. And that lad was born in Wakefield. It makes a Yorkshireman think that these things might be better arranged.

The 1955 match was an interesting example of a theory of mine. Your ideal spectator always has two notions in his mind : he wants to see his own side win and he wants to see the game played as excellently as it can be played. There are some who claim that they do not care who wins so long as it is a good game. It may be so. I think that if I were watching, say, Warwickshire v. Worcestershire, with neither of which I have any affiliations, I could adopt an impartial attitude, but sooner or later I should remember that I was a long-term admirer of Tom Dollery or perhaps of Reg Perks, and then bang would go objectivity. To be without prejudice is an admirable attitude, no doubt, but somehow it is possible to suspect its sincerity. If I were watching a match played between penguins of the north pole and penguins of the south pole, I should shout like mad for the north, if only to warm the game up a bit. The man that hath no partisanship in his soul is fit for treasons, stratagems and spoils; let no such man be trusted. Having said that, I readily agree that the other thing is important, too.

The 1955 game ministered to both my prejudices. It was alive all the time; there was some excellent bowling and fielding and, after a doughty battle, Yorkshire won. Middlesex's first innings was a sandwich : two slices of mouldy bread with caviare in the middle. Robertson was out early, Brown struggled conscientiously along, Edrich made a run or two, and then Delisle joined Denis Compton. The Oxford man batted pugnaciously but Compton touched the heights. There is still only one Denis Compton, though he is not always to be seen in a golden light. On his day, and his days were frequent in 1955, there are rainbows round his shoulder. That afternoon he batted like one of the shining company. I, who saw Trumper twice, and Ranji several times, tell you this. Before he came in, the Yorkshire attack had been sharp and relentless. When he began to operate upon it, it ceased to be an attack. The fiery Trueman, the wily Wardle : where was their sting, where was their victory?

He cut them, he pulled them, he danced impudently down the pitch and either drove them gloriously over the bowlers' head or, in sheer effrontery, glanced them to fine leg. It seemed impossible to bowl a length to him. Nor, apart from his straight drives, did he usually appear to hit the ball with violence; more often it looked as if he stroked, persuaded, caressed . . . It was only when the ball hit the pavilion rails with a venomous crack that you realised it had been struck at all. Such was the completeness of his command that you felt that the bat itself was superfluous. Only a gesture seemed necessary. He had only to point good-naturedly to the boundary and thither the ball flew. That innings was rich in those 'delicate and elaborate ingenuities of form and style' which so delighted Sir Max Beerbohm in literature. It was impossible to watch it without being bemused and enchanted; it was something of which boys who saw it would tell their grandsons and would be told not to exaggerate. When he was out, caught in the slips by Wardle off a lofty mishit, the glory departed and Trueman rolled up the rest of the innings like a dusty hearthrug. In the event, Yorkshire gained a fifty-odd lead, Lowson batted like the *petit maitre* he is and then Appleyard took six for 51 in a devastating attack. Yorkshire won comfortably by eight wickets and so, not for the first time, I had had it both ways. I had seen victory come to the 'right' side and I had witnessed some batting that no man has a right to expect to see more than once in a lifetime. The fact that this came from the 'wrong' side is just too bad.

IV

The first Middlesex v. Yorkshire game I ever saw was in 1910, which was odd, because I did not officially invade the metropolis until two years later. I went up to London in June 1910 in order to suffer an examination, which was to decide whether, when I was old enough, I should become a member of a university or not. This essentially unimportant question eventually settled itself, but that is another story. When the ordeal by pen and paper was over, there was still a day of happy freedom left, because matches then ended on a Saturday instead of beginning on one. When I made my way across the road to Lord's from the old St. John's Wood Road station, I had already visited the Zoo and Madame Tussaud's and located (at any rate to my own satisfaction) the putative residence of Sherlock Holmes. Looking back, I still think this was excellent value for a Yorkshire lad's Saturday morning in the Baker Street area. As I passed through the turnstile, I had no idea that I should see the most exciting finish of the year. I was not interested in what afterwards came to be called 'thrills.' I only wanted to see my heroes.

Now any north-country boy could admire his heroes at Headingley, Park Avenue or Bramall Lane, but there, on their home grounds, he had to share them with the rest of the crowd. But on that day at Lord's, the great ones were my exclusive property, all eleven of them. The crowd were merely Londoners. Hirst and Rhodes, Denton and Haigh were not theirs; Yorkshire belonged to me. With the help of a penny score-card and two Cockney neighbours I was able to assess the situation. In strict fact, my neighbours were not Cockney; one came from Frognal and the other from Finchley. But to me anyone born south-east of a line drawn between Arnold Bennett and Thomas Hardy was a Cockney. To do them justice, they on their side probably thought that anyone born north of Finsbury Park was a Lancashire comedian.

At any rate they were most helpful and informative. It appeared that, despite some cunning bowling by Rhodes the previous afternoon, Yorkshire had been set the awkward task of getting 331 runs in the fourth innings and were making none too good a job of it. Up to then they had lost three wickets for under 50. The three who had gone were all good men: Rhodes himself who was now Yorkshire's and soon to become England's No. 2; Jimmy Rothery, my fellow-towns-man, and Wilkinson, W. H., a steady left-hander, not to be confused with H. Wilkinson, also my fellow-townsman. My new acquaintances informed me sympathetically that York-shire did not have a dog's chance.

Poised between a fluttering hope and that natural north-country pessimism that knows enough not to ask Providence for too much, I watched the pitch intently. At the wicket I could see David Denton, with his cavalier air and cavalry moustache. (Years afterwards he shaved it off and, though he batted as well as ever, he never looked quite the same again.) The other batsman had not yet arrived at the wicket, but was striding towards it from the pavilion gate. No need to ask the identity of that stocky, deep-chested, square-shoul-dered figure. It was George Hirst. The cheers with which the crowd greeted him gave me a momentary pang of jealousy. After all, he was my Hirst, not theirs. But immediately after-wards I realised the fact that should have been obvious before. Any reasonably popular player may be warmly welcomed on his own grounds, but Hirst and Rhodes were different. They lived their cricketing lives upon a wider stage under a brighter limelight. They were greeted with affectionate ad-

miration everywhere they went, not merely at Leeds and
Sheffield, but here at Lord's, the Oval, Old Trafford and
Trent Bridge. Everybody knew them and everybody cheered
them; their friends were innumerable, especially among their
hereditary enemies.

The situation was critical and there have always been two
ways of dealing with such a crisis. One is to put up the
shutters, sit on the splice, and, with a dour, grim, back-to-
the-wall expression, stun every ball into insensibility till the
clock says six-thirty. This is the method once employed by
J. W. H. T. Douglas and now adopted, in almost fossilized
form, by Trevor Bailey, whom heaven preserve.

It is a worthy method, dictated by what Milton calls 'bitter
constraint and sad occasion dear.' But the other, at least in
the sight of the gods that rule over cricket, is a better way
and it is a way that appealed to Hirst and Denton. These
two, bearing the burden of their responsibility with lightness
of heart, played as if this was a Saturday afternoon, as indeed
it was. You would not have thought that they had a care in
the world. Picking out the right ball to hit, Hirst pulled it to
the leg-side boundary with a kind of genial fury. Denton also
picked out the right ball to hit. There seemed to be at least
five of them in every over. There was the right ball to cut, the
right ball to hook and the right ball to hit for four straight
back to the sight-screen. The crowd, as I have always found
in the forty-odd years since that day, were generous in their
applause, and for the best of reasons : they knew grand cricket
when they saw it. Denton was out at last, caught by a short
young man with a mischievous expression, whose wholly im-
plausible name was Elias P. Hendren. But when Denton went,
he and Hirst had put on over 160 and the question was no
longer one of saving the game but of challenging the clock.

I wish you could have seen the way Hirst farmed the bowling; it was a triumph of planned agriculture; or, to vary the
metaphor, his devotion in shepherding his weaker brethren
away from the rigours of the bowling was a supreme example
of pastoral care. A hundred were needed. Then sixty. While
Hirst was in, the match was alight and burning brightly.
When he was out, leg-before-wicket for 137, it seemed that
the flame would fade. Hubert Myers, that sturdy all-rounder,
began to 'steal' the bowling as Hirst had 'stolen' it. Wickets

fell and my hopes sank with them. Alonzo Drake, the most promising left-handed recruit of the season, came and went. So did Newstead, one of Yorkshire's rare all-rounders from the North Riding. So did E. J. Radcliffe, who had taken over the captaincy that season from Lord Hawke. And still Yorkshire did not shut up shop.

When Schofield Haigh came in, it was twenty-five past six by my five-shilling watch, a massive timepiece specifically bought—one might almost have said minted—for my visit to the metropolis. The conduct of the crowd was a model of what crowd behaviour should be; no film executive could have directed it more skilfully. Silent as each ball was bowled, they broke into a roar with each hit. My watch said six-thirty as the last over began, though the thumping beneath the waistcoat pocket where it lay may have set it fast. Eight runs were needed; two wickets might fall; Yorkshire could draw, lose or win. That over was almost suspended in time and every ball, though I did not know the expression at the time, seemed to be delivered in slow motion. Off the fifth ball of the over Myers made the winning hit. The crowd's applause boiled over, and for a long time they stood in, or on, their seats, cheering the players as they finally retreated to the pavilion.

It is pompously said that art has no frontiers. Cricket, which I hold to be a high if modest art, has frontiers of partisanship in plenty. But the magnanimity evoked by a hard-fought victory or a brave defeat transcends all everyday barriers. I saluted the large heartedness of the enemy and I went back happily to Yorkshire on the night train, not caring whether I had won a scholarship or not and not even knowing it would have been better for me if I hadn't.

V

Do not, however, quote me as saying that all the palpitating finishes occurred in the old days. Far from it. There was one a couple of years ago and its hero was Wardle, J. H., that ebullient personality whose whole existence is a daily denial of the contention that there are no characters in the game nowadays. No doubt old gentlemen made the same complaint in Tom Emmett's day.

It was one of those slightly daft games in which captains
are continually pitting their wits against each other's and
declaring all over the place. It was also Jim Sims's second
benefit and I could happily attend a third. Yorkshire started
off at breathless speed, declaring at 437 for six after a swift,
evenly-spread innings which contained two seventies, two sixties, a fifty and a 44 not out. Then Middlesex, after a sedate
opening partnership of nearly 200, fell unaccountably to
pieces and had only saved the follow-on by the skin of their
teeth when the ninth wicket fell.

At this point Robins, the Middlesex captain, displaying
his own particular brand of high-hearted impudence, declared
his innings closed exactly 149 runs behind and now it was
Yorkshire who were dared to have a go. Yardley rose to the
challenge as he has always done. Swift scoring was of the
essence; if 'twere well done, 'twere well 'twere done quickly.
The order of the day was to hit out or get out and Yorkshiremen obeyed it loyally. Lowson drove splendidly in a style
reminiscent of his master, Hutton; several others collected a
quick dozen runs or so apiece and departed. Then Wardle
made his entry and if he had been accompanied to the wicket
by a rendering of Handel's *Music for the Royal Fireworks,* the
background noises would not have been inappropriate. Bang,
bang, bang, *bang.* His 40 contained four rasping fours and a
glorious six and the ball was lucky to have a cover left when
he had finished with it. Royal fireworks, indeed . . .

Now it was Yardley's turn to declare and Robins's turn to
say in effect : ' All right, come on then, watch us get 'em . . .'
He went in first himself, instead of No. 7, and began by
emulating Wardle's fireworks, lashing away until he lashed
once too often at the empty air and Brennan whipped the
bails off. After that, Wardle took charge of the attack and,
with a kindly smile on his face, hewed Middlesex in pieces
like Agag, King of the Amalekites. Jim Sims, that affable old
warrior, offered an amiable clout or two, but otherwise there
was no serious resistance movement. Wardle laid them gently
to rest and their end was peaceful. His bowling figures were
eight for 26, and though each season since then a conscientious
search has been conducted for a better slow bowler, no one
can claim that it has been wholly successful.

VI

Perhaps I have omitted the most important Yorkshireman who ever played at Lord's. He was a North Riding man, from the Thirsk district and, like the great John Nyren himself, he was a member of an old Catholic family that had suffered for its loyalty to the Young Chevalier. The family moved south, first to Norfolk and then to London, where he found a job as attendant at a gentlemen's club. Part of his duty was to bowl to the members, and he helped to organise the matches that they played in fields near the pretty village of Islington.

A little later two aristocratic members of the club who were also patrons of cricket suggested to our Yorkshireman that, with their backing, he should lay out a new ground. This he did and the first big match, one of those county games played for a large money stake, took place in June 1787. This ground had a comparatively but literally short lease of life: he was obliged to change its site twice; the first time, twenty-two years later and the second five years later still. On each occasion he moved the turf so that the third ground had exactly the same surface as the first and, despite the passage of nearly a century and a half, some of it may, for all I know, be the same still.

He stayed in the neighbourhood for many years, became a pillar of local government, had a prosperous business in wines and spirits and finally, at the age of seventy-four, he retired to Hampshire where he died two years later. That he was a Yorkshireman is confirmed by the fact that he was the first man ever to charge the public sixpence to watch a cricket match.

His name was Thomas Lord.

CHAPTER 3

HERE ARE SOUTH AFRICANS

I

IT IS always delightful to meet South Africans. I visited their country a good many years ago, not, unfortunately, for the purpose of playing cricket, but in the course of a journey towards one of the sillier fronts of the first world war; in South Africa I had the pleasure of climbing Table Mountain, smoking Afrikander tobacco (which you carried in a canvas bag tied to your belt), eating oranges straight off the tree, cautiously surveying an ostrich farm, riding in a rickshaw drawn by a Zulu chieftain in gleaming warpaint and horned headdress, and drinking a pleasant variety of Cape wines, not to mention a rather taking liqueur called Van der Hum.

These were all highly stimulating experiences and, whenever I recall them, I think of South Africans as lively and warm-hearted hosts. It is equally certain that, as cricketers, they are colourful and good-natured guests. Right from the beginnings of the game in their country it was recorded of the South Africans that they treated cricket 'as a game, not as a business, and played it on all occasions in the best possible spirit . . .'

This was true when it was first spoken and it has been true of every South African team to visit these shores from the first visitors of 1894 to those of 1901 and 1904; and then on, from the first to be given Test match status (in 1907) to the quick-footed combination under J. E. Cheetham which blossomed into life and colour under English sunshine forty-eight years later. In all those visits, covering well over half a century, there may have been an occasional weaker side, as in 1912, but never a really dull one. Three qualities have been continuously woven into the pattern of their play; vigorous (or extremely stubborn) batting; bowling of almost infinite variety, especially during the era of the googly kings, and, above all, fielding that is a pure joy to watch and must be a joy to execute.

Bear with me. I have a *thing* about fielding. Of all the delights of cricket, it can give the greatest pleasure, both to do and to watch being done. It blesses him that gives and him that spectates. Conversely, bad fielding is the evil thing. I am normally a friendly soul, tolerant to the point of foolishness towards human frailties, if only because I have so many of my own. But sloppy, couldn't-care-less, don't-bother-to-stoop fielding freezes the genial current of my soul. It is very nearly the authentic unpardonable sin. In 1953, when Yorkshire fell from grace and lay depressingly low—practically on the ocean bed—in the county table, there was no doubt as to the root of their trouble. George Hirst's comment, coming from the kindest of men, was sterner than any profane rebuke. ' They tell me Yorkshire are fielding badly,' he said and added, in classic phrase : ' *This is not news I like to hear . . .*' Happily there was a visible improvement the following year and still more pleasing advance the year after, so that, in 1955 the county's fielding was *sans peur* close to the wicket and *sans reproche* anywhere else.

The fielding of the 1955 South Africans was handsome in the extreme, and an object lesson to cricketers everywhere. Their reputation was of the highest and when A. G. Moyes, that robust Australian commentator, first saw them play, he said : ' I was struck at once by their glorious fielding, their physical fitness, youth and vigour, and strict attention to the job in hand—playing cricket for South Africa.' You had only to watch them in the field for five minutes to realise how well their good name had been deserved, and how strongly they were determined not to let it slip. Furthermore, to their efficiency they added grace.

Perfection in fielding involves several qualities, including a nearly fanatical degree of physical fitness, a jet-propelled quickness off the mark and an extra anticipatory sense that gives an uncanny impression that the ball is going straight to the man.

I watched this with mingled pleasure and exasperation in the Lord's Test of 1955, which England, I thought at the time, were rather lucky to win. The contrast between the

South African and the English fielding was a joy to watch—
for a South African. When England fielded, there were
obvious gaps in the cordon; with the Springboks, there was
not a gap anywhere. I counted the players, but there were
only eleven. The impression that there were two or three extra
fieldsmen, each with two or three extra arms and legs, was
erroneous, though strong. I know it was an optical illusion,
but there were moments when England seemed to have only
five or six men in the field while South Africa had fifteen or
sixteen.

When McLean, that flashing, quick-footed hitter, was facing the bowling, the whole of the off-side seemed wide open.
Four followed four : he seemed to cut and drive them anywhere and as often as he liked. But when the positions were
reversed and England were batting, the picture was sadly
different. Here you could see May, a finer bat than McLean,
and Graveney, on his day an equally aggressive one; and
yet, splendid as their strokes were, time after time they were
cut off by McLean. The fact is that, when McLean was
guarding the covers, he stopped the fours; when he was
batting, nobody could stop them.

These young South Africans, before arriving on these shores,
had already succeeded during the winter of 1953-54 in winning half a Test series on Australian grounds, not by great
batting, not by great bowling, except from one man, but by
the simple, if heroic, expedient of taking every catch that
came to hand and a number of vital ones that did not even
do that. As for the contention that they were the finest fielding
side ever to set foot in England, this seems a tallish claim
to those who saw Clarence Pellew and his fellow Australians
in 1921, but by this, the highest standard I can think of, they
were very fine indeed. Their captain said that in England
they did not field quite so well as they had in Australia,
but that only makes their Australian fielding seem more
miraculous.

What was their secret ? I do not know, but it was plain that
they fielded as a side, which no recent English eleven has
ever quite been able to do. True, there are dazzling specialists,
such as Evans and Lock, but the Springboks comprised a perfectly integrated streamlined machine in which seven or eight
specialists, each of whom was as brilliant as England's best,

performed a supreme task individually and collectively. Seldom in this unsatisfactory world does one hundred per cent efficiency go hand in hand with sheer delight. When Cheetham's Springboks were in the field, these two virtues positively embraced.

II

' Happy ' and ' enterprising ' are, I think, adjectives that can be fairly applied to South African batting over a long period. There have been batsmen who have been solid, like Dudley Nourse, Eric Rowan, as well as T. L. Goddard and H. J. Keith, the 1955 left-handers. Dudley Nourse, son of David Nourse, the stubborn old warrior of an older generation, earned golden opinions for his 208 in the Nottingham Test of 1951, where his physical and mental courage stuck out literally like a sore thumb. He was at the wicket for over nine hours and the pain from his fractured left thumb must have made every stroke an agony.

South Africa has had her stolid batsmen, too, like Bruce Mitchell, whose broad bat broke many a bowler's proud spirit. Frequently he would save South Africa as the little Dutch boy saved the dyke, and with as little motion. It is recorded that once, after being at the wicket for about five hours, he looked up in sudden surprise at his partner and said : ' Hullo, when did you come in?' South Africa, too, has produced batsmen of true elegance in style, like Alan Melville, captain of the 1947 touring side, and, more glorious than all, at least one player of classic magnificence.

This was H. W. (Herbie) Taylor, who found a place in South African sides from 1912 to 1929. His admirers, and these included all who bowled against him, claimed that he was in a world-eleven class by himself. Without doubt he was one of the very few batsmen of the period who could play the great Sidney Barnes with confidence and mastery. In the Test matches of England's 1913-14 tour of South Africa, Barnes's bowling was a nightmare to successive home sides. Barnes dominated South Africa, but Taylor dominated Barnes. In the rather unhappy triangular tournament of 1912, the wettest summer between Noah and 1954, everybody had the worst of the weather and the South Africans, with five

C

defeats, had the worst of the deal. Throughout all this, Taylor kept the flag flying. To watch him batting on a bad wicket was to see again some of the regal splendour of an innings by A. C. MacLaren.

The exploits of the Springboks in the delectable English summer of 1955 still linger with us and from many of their batsmen we received a god's plenty of enterprise, colour and entertainment. The redoubtable McGlew pugnaciously headed the season's batting averages, Endean and Waite at need performed sturdy feats of fortitude and Winslow put on occasional pyrotechnic displays which gave pleasure to everyone except the bowlers undergoing treatment. Sometimes a visit to the wicket by Winslow was not so much an innings as a punitive expedition. In his last Australian tour Endean made more runs than Hutton, May or Cowdrey did on theirs and in the English tour half a dozen Springboks cheerfully made a thousand runs. No English spectators could complain that they did not receive entertainment-value for their money. And, of course, there was Tayfield, but that brings us to the bowling.

III

South African bowling has always had a special interest of its own, for connoisseurs as well as discomfited batsmen, and the word 'googly' instantly comes to mind. Why 'googly'? Why not? When Tom Emmett was asked why he called his most devastating ball a 'sostenutor,' he replied socratically : 'Why, what else would you call it?' The South Africans were not the inventors of the googly; the only begetter of that immortal and, as he himself called it, immoral ball was B. J. T. Bosanquet, the illustrious 'Bose,' whose bewildering bowling was a main cause of the recovery of the Ashes by P. F. Warner's 1903-04 tourists. The Australians were bowled by it, caught off mishits from it, stumped from rushing maniacally down the pitch to it and, by and large, were completely flummoxed by it.

The South Africans of 1907 brought with them a more intimidating gaggle of googly-merchants than has ever plagued batsmen at one time before or since. Among them were R. O. Schwarz (also a Rugby footballer), A. E. Vogler, G. A. Faulk-

ner and Gordon White. And for good measure, they cocked a
couple of Snookes (S. J. and S. D.) at the English, too. At first
the googly was defined as an off-break with a leg-break
action. But it was more than that. It was a ball that might
break one way or the other, generally the other, only you
could never tell which. From the fast pitches of South Africa
it naturally came off very fast, but the alarming fact to
English batsmen was that from the slow, wet English pitches
it came off (or appeared to come off) just as quickly. I am
always being told that this is mathematically and physically
impossible, but I am more willing to believe the old cricketer
who indignantly asserted that, when you faced a googly, it
was like playing ' Briggs through the air and Tom Rirchard-
son off the pitch.' In the modern idiom, one might similarly
ask : how would you like to deal with a bowler who could
wrap up all the cunning of a Wardle and the ferocity of a
Trueman in one delivery? No doubt acceleration off the pitch
is ' impossible.' It is also ' impossible ' that a world-famous
batsman should be cozened by an innocent-looking ball, but
it happens.

Schwarz in 1907 headed the season's bowling averages with
nearly 150 wickets at a cost of 11.51 apiece, but Vogler was
reckoned an even more skilful practitioner of the ' wrong
'un.' His special delivery was like an O. Henry story : you
knew exactly what was going to happen and then something
else happened altogether. With this ball he twice in Test
matches clean bowled C. B. Fry, who may well be reckoned
the most vigilant, and indeed the most nearly invincible, evil-
wicket batsman of his period. Faulkner and White were
throughout the season almost as dangerous, particularly
Faulkner. One of the finest all-round cricketers in the history
of the game, he chose the great occasion to be great, and
never more so than in the Test at Leeds.

In another chapter I shall speak, with some emotion, of
some of the horrid happenings that occur when England plays
at Leeds. For English cricketers the road to Headingley has
been as perilous as the ancient biblical road to Jericho. In
1907 England won the toss, batted first, and fell like ninepins
to Faulkner, who took six for 17 in what was plainly one of
the most splendid performances even of his career. Only
Hayward, Tyldesley and Hirst reached double figures. Even

then, a strong and courageous England eleven fought their way back. What was unlucky for South Africa was that they then came up against Colin Blythe who was, always excepting Wilfred Rhodes, the best slow bowler who ever lived. Blythe pulled out of the bag an even more baffling and spectacular display than Faulkner, taking fifteen wickets for fewer than a hundred runs. This was the only Test in the series which, owing to weather and one thing and another, managed to reach a finish. Thanks to providence and Colin Blythe, England won it, but the South Africans had made their mark with a wider and more satisfied public than they had ever reached before. That public will still welcome a South African side whenever they appear.

The unluckiest of South Africa's bowlers was Athol Rowan, brother of the high-scoring Eric, who for a long time had the reputation of being very nearly the best off-spinner of his time, and it could be argued that he was never truly mastered. He damaged his knee and was forced to retire from cricket at the end of the 1951 tour, a sad conclusion to a talented and happy career.

Hugh (Toey) Tayfield was in his early days regarded as a mild shadow of Athol Rowan, but both at home and in his last two tours he has come to the fore as South Africa's key man, the Springbok's indispensable. On Australian and English grounds countless spectators have watched and even waited for his queer toe-stubbing action when bowling and, quite often, when batting. How conscious this action now is it is hard to say. I have heard that the stubbing began one day when, as a schoolboy, he borrowed his father's cricket boots. They were much too big for him and he kept jabbing his toes to force them further into the toe of the boot. Whatever the reason, he jabbed his way through Australian and English sides and it was certainly not through any failure of his that England snatched the rubber in 1955. In this Test series he and Goddard took 51 wickets between them, which was six more than the three most destructive English bowlers took altogether. His length throughout the tour was as persistent as toothache and he will, I believe, live to be a headache to English batsmen for many a day.

South African bowling has naturally not been confined to the googly. The Springboks have had their thunders and their lightnings, too. As we recently saw, there were Adcock and Heine who, if they had been laid end to end, which is what the English batsmen who were their victims must have wished to do, would have stretched very little short of thirteen feet. These two in England acquitted themselves manfully and with due fierceness, though it was Heine, originally the second string, who was in the event the more penetrative of the two. Earlier than this, on the 1951 tour, there was Cuan McCarthy, the tall Cambridge undergraduate with the high muzzle-velocity and the double-jointed wrist-flicking action which caused umpires to give him an occasional old-fashioned look. Against Sussex at Hove he took eight for 14 at a pace which made the batsmen feel that some evil from a hostile planet had befallen them.

Earlier still, while there was nobody of devastating pace in 1947, we saw Crisp and Langton in 1935, but if you wanted to see the authentic lightning streaking across the sky, you would have to hark back once more to the famous 1907 side which, besides the googly men, contained one truly tear-away attacker, J. J. Kotze.

This colourful character had a whirling windmill action and was probably as fast as the very fastest, Kortright, Knox, Larwood or any of the other projectors of guided missiles. The wet season was a handicap to a man of his speed, as was also the fact that Schwarz, Vogler or Faulkner had generally broken down the enemy's defences before he was called on. But on his matting wicket at home, he was a holy terror. There is a legend that, as he came pounding up to the wicket to deliver his atomic projectile, he could be heard breathing a supplication to heaven to scatter his enemies' stumps to the four winds. That prayer, alas for England, was frequently answered.

IV

Besides being noted for their googly bowlers, the South Africans have made a frequent habit of producing wicket-keepers who are batsmen in their own right. In the early days of the century there was E. A. Halliwell, who miraculously stood up to Kotze, which was about the most daring act in history since Ajax defied the lightning. Some may attribute this recklessness to what Dr. Johnson called 'sheer insensibility,' but for sheer courage, at least, I believe that it places him in the immortal ranks of Blackham and Gregor McGregor. A little later there was P. W. Sherwell, hero of South Africa's first victory over England, who was as good a wicket-keeper as Halliwell and a better bat. This victory was won at Johannesburg in England's 1905-06 tour. It was a win by one wicket in a finish where excitement mounted minute by minute and Sherwell made the winning hit, story-book fashion, as the clock struck. Sir Pelham Warner has said that it was the best match he ever played in and he must have rated it very high indeed, for he had a rich selection to choose from.

And there was H. B. Cameron, that gay, vivid and mercurial character who, alas, died young. In the Lord's Test of 1935, I saw him hammer the English bowlers virtually into insensibility. With me was a well-known musical conductor and his behaviour-pattern (if that is the right expression) during Cameron's innings was a study for a psychologist. He was an Englishman, nay, a Yorkshireman, and he could not endure to see English bowlers, especially Verity, treated so cavalierly. As the fours swept from Cameron's bat, radiating all round the wicket almost like electric flashes, his brow darkened and his fingers drummed a disapproving tattoo on the boundary rail in front of him. But, though he was an Englishman, he was also an artist; as the power and beauty of Cameron's stroke-play dawned on him and warmed him his internal tensions relaxed; by the time Cameron's score had reached eighty, my friend had frankly abandoned all restraint and was playing lyrical arpeggios, as on a harp, along the railings. It was Cameron, you remember, who in an earlier match of the tour against Yorkshire was the cause of Arthur Wood's deathless observation to Hedley Verity: 'You've got him in two minds; he doesn't know whether to hit you for four or six!' Now both Cameron and Verity have gone from us and cricket is infinitely the poorer.

Not merely did South Africa specialise in finding the odd wicket-keeper batsman; in 1955 they were capable of bringing out of the hat no less than three: Waite, a stubborn bat, who has filled most of the early positions from one to six, but has a penchant for running himself out even more alarming than

Denis Compton's; Endean, who kept wicket in 1951, but was more valuable in other fielding positions in 1955; and Duckworth, the reserve wicket-keeper, a young schoolmaster who in county games showed his ability to hit sixes in the best academic traditions.

Waite's heart-stopping miscalculations between wickets, I have been told, first arose when his partners kept appearing to call him for impossible runs. What they said, of course, was: 'Wait!' When I saw him in the second innings of the final Test at the Oval, he bore the brunt of England's spin attack, whence all but he, one might almost say, had fled. When five wickets had fallen on a tricky pitch for less than sixty, he played as though conditions were easy, driving hard to leg and showing the traditional off-side strokes in all their splendour. As for his running between the wickets, it was faultless. Like Tayfield he could accept no blame for the Springboks' defeat.

Perhaps, most of all, South Africa has been the cradle of all-rounders, including J. H. Sinclair, their mightiest hitter, and Aubrey Faulkner, their greatest batsman-bowler, and indeed one of the greatest in any country in any age. The 1955 side had a more varied batch of all-rounders than has come to England for a long time and, what was more, most of them acquitted themselves admirably. They were proud rather than ashamed of being all-rounders, and that, in this age of over-specialisation, was something to warm the heart.

CHAPTER 4

SEND THEM VICTORIOUS

I

I F YOU reckon James Lillywhite's intrepid band of twelve adventurers who visited Australia and New Zealand in 1876-77 to be the first 'real' touring side to do the journey, then, if I can count correctly (and the statisticians distrust me to a man) England has sent out twenty-two sides, teams, bodies, combinations or outfits towards the Southern Cross and nine of them have come back carrying the trophies of victory. There have been many differences in quality and even in quantity between these sides : some, as has become the recent custom, have been rather large; others, like Lilly-white's were alarmingly small. Some played one, two or three Test matches; later sides have played the now statutory five. Most were captained by amateurs; a few, of which Hutton's was not the only one, were captained by professionals. Alfred Shaw and Arthur Shrewsbury commanded the invasions of the 1880's and proved themselves to be as provident in management as in bowling and batting.

One thing, however, the winning sides had in common. I will not state categorically that each of them was separately and individually the worst team ever to leave these shores, except Warner's side of 1903-04, and, of course, Hutton's of 1954-55, but all in greater or lesser degree were subjected to abuse by those to whom all wisdom had been vouchsafed from heaven, but who did not have the selectors' responsibilities and would not have to face the Australians' bowling.

I have often thought that the more a side is criticised before it leaves England, the better chance of success it has before it comes back and then the abuse seems to matter very little. When things had reached the red-carpet-and-brass-bands-in-Pudsey stage, Hutton's severely criticised combination had hardly a detractor in the world. The critics were rather like the post-war Germans who turned out to have been anti-Nazi all along in such numbers that one wondered how Hitler ever managed to scrape up any support at all. Everybody rallied to Hutton's side when he came home in triumph. Give me the man who was on Hutton's side after the first disastrous Test at Brisbane, when everything went wrong that could go wrong, and much more besides. At that point the pundits were practically unanimous in their orders to send the whole lot home and call it a day. This was their finest hour. They were prepared to censure Hutton severely if he lost the toss and even more severely if he failed to lose it. But from that moment things began to fail to go wrong.

II

If I do not wax lyrical about England's first three successful 'rubbers'—they were certainly not called rubbers then—it is because the information about them is a trifle sketchy. In 1884-85 a professional team, led by England's second greatest batsman of the period, Arthur Shrewsbury, and managed by him jointly with England's greatest contemporary bowler, Alfred Shaw, carried off the prize in true storybook fashion, winning the first two games, losing the third and fourth and then finishing strongly with an innings victory in the fifth. The side was immensely strong for those early touring days, and its outstanding players seemed to come from either Yorkshire or Notts. George Ulyett and Billy Bates of Yorkshire and William Barnes of Notts were only three of its all-rounders, while Bobby Peel (Yorks) and W. Attewell (Notts) were but two of its bowlers; Shrewsbury himself— 'Give me Arthur!'—and W. (Billy) Bates the most successful batsmen. With both bat and ball William Barnes did wonders. The irrepressible Bobby Peel had a bag of 353 wickets over the whole tour at just over five runs each. Even if some of these were against eighteens and twenty-twos, the result is still fantastic.

In 1886-87 Shrewsbury took out a similar and even slightly stronger side, reinforced by Surrey's immaculate young bowler, George Lohmann. Only two Tests were played, both at Sydney and both won by England. In the first game England were practically put up against a wall and shot for 45,

but, after a breathlessly low-scoring game, they scraped home
by 13 runs. The second was also a bowlers' carnival and a
game of low scores, in which Australia might have just held
their own if Lohmann, with eight wickets for 35, had not
ruined their chances.

England's third victorious visit was an odd affair, because
two touring teams were in Australia at the same time and
only one Test match was arranged. One English side was
led by Lord Hawke and the other by C. A. (later Sir Aubrey,
but then known as Round the Corner) Smith. I am not sure
where they met or how they managed it, but, for the single
Test, they picked a single team. Walter Read captained it for
the occasion and some superb bowling, first by Lohmann and
then by Peel (who in all took ten for 58), put the enemy to
complete rout. Once more it was a low-scoring game and
Shrewsbury's 40 was reckoned a mighty total. He also took
half a dozen slip catches. After that the Test side broke up
and the players went on with their respective tours as if
nothing had happened.

III

I do not know if you could call A. E. Stoddart's team of
1894-95 the harbinger of Hutton's sixty years later, but it
won a tight rubber, which a side captained by W. G. Grace
in all his glory had failed to do three winters before. Stoddart's men, like Shrewsbury's, ended the series in victory,
by taking the last game after winning two Tests and losing
two, while the first of their games ran out into one of the
most palpitating of all Test match finishes.

It is an oft-told tale how Australia, winning the toss on a
pitch more suited to snooker than bowling, piled up a huge
total. There were early shocks when Tom Richardson gloriously bowled the first three Australian batsmen for next
to nothing. Then, though honest Tom toiled and sweated
under the Sydney sun, there was a stand of immense length
between Giffen and Iredale and again between Giffen and
Syd Gregory, who made 201. Towards the end of the ordeal,
with all the bowlers except Richardson begging for mercy,
Blackham at No. 10 cruelly hammered out 74, but in the
finish Tom bowled him and the Australian total was 586.

England started feebly and shuffled along with little fight from anybody except Lancashire's Yorkshireman, Albert Ward. It was the tail-enders, Brockwell and Briggs, who hauled England back to the respectable figure of 325. Disgrace was avoided but the follow-on was not. In the second innings Ward was still the defiant warrior and this time he received sounder support from J. T. Brown, Brockwell, Lockwood and Briggs. Even Richardson made a dozen, a good score for Tom.

Despite this fighting recovery, Australia were left with only 187 to win and when stumps were drawn on the third evening, they had scored 113 for two. Their task was easy, their burden light. It was, as the Australians might have said, money for IXL. There was rain in the night and the sun in the morning, and the gods sent a wicket that was a boon to Briggs and a paradise for Peel. George Giffen says in his memoirs : ' The first man I met outside was Blackham with a face as long as a coffee-pot.' And well it might be. The ball behaved like a jumping cracker. The Australians, struggling vainly against what must have looked to them like black magic, faded away and incredibly lost this incredible game by ten runs. Of the eight wickets that fell for 53 that horrible sunny morning, Bobby Peel took five and he little knew then what he was going to pay for it.

The second game was almost as exciting. It was England's turn to bat on a foul fiend's pitch. On what was then for the first time called a ' Melbourne sticky dog,' England were put in and unceremoniously bundled out again in almost record time for 75. The wicket had become kinder by the time the Australians went in but not kind enough to give them a decent score. Fast and slow bowling came alike to them. It was all very difficult, with Richardson (five for 57) hardest of all. England's score in their second innings was an imposing one, erected round the structure of a massive 173 by Stoddart, and his men built steadily with him, brick by brick. Tom Richardson, as he had done at Sydney, made double figures. Australia were left 428 to get to win. Their efforts, especially those of Trott, Bruce and Iredale, were stupendous; their failure, by less than a hundred runs, was gallant indeed. And so England were two up.

This is a stage at which Australia, cornered and at bay, are at their most dangerous. (It was out of this pit that they climbed and slew G. O. Allen's men in 1936-37.) For the third time Australia won the toss. On this occasion they batted first, led by 114 runs on the first innings and then set England an almost impossible total to overhaul. The task was rendered completely impossible by the bowling of a newcomer, Albert Trott, younger brother of the better-known G.H.S. England must have wondered what had struck them. In the first innings he made 32 not out and in the second 82 not out. They could not cope with his bowling and his eight for 43 must have made them feel that they were suffering from some seismic disturbance. England lost by 382 runs and Bobby Peel bagged a brace. Of Richardson's pluck in this match, Giffen speaks almost with awe. ' With the broiling sun streaming on the back of his curly black hair, and the intense heat trying him severely, he bowled like a veritable demon . . .'

The fourth game brought a further shock; Australia, put in on a rain-soaked wicket, made the best of it while it was wet and then summarily dismissed England twice upon it while it was drying. The scores were 65 and 72 and life must have seemed very hard. Albert Trott, afterwards to be Middlesex's most vivid all-rounder, made 82 not out. (Could nobody ever get him out?) As for bowling, Giffen, Turner, and the elder Trott did pretty much as they liked. And Peel acquired his second ' pair,' stumped both times, leaping out, I imagine, in a fury of sheer exasperation.

The last Test was the decider, the most acute of needle games. The wicket was a glossy shirt-front and Stoddart for the fourth time lost the toss. Australia were bound to score heavily and score they did. Gregory and Giffen contributed their usual quota and another youngster, left-handed Joe Darling, hacked his way to 74. England's reply to this total of 414 was heroic. There was a majestic 120 from the young A. C. MacLaren, while Peel and Stoddart proved themselves good for 70-odd apiece. With a lead of 29 Australia, despite some spirited defiance from Giffen, made only 267. They did, however, capture one wicket—it was Brockwell's—for 28 by close of play on the fourth evening, and to the first ball sent down on the following morning Stoddart was out l.b.w.

England were up against it. At one end was Albert Ward, steady as a cliff or a Trevor Bailey; to the other came J. T.

Brown, thinking perhaps of his career-long partner, Tunnicliffe, now sitting at home at ease in Pudsey, far from the
rigours of Melbourne's heat and drama. While Ward continued to present a broad bat and an unbroken front, Brown
batted like an archangel. Sober Australians have put it on
record that he batted like Trumper three years before Trumper
had seriously been heard of. By the time the patient Ward (93)
and the dazzling Brown (140) were out, the back of the task
was broken and, amid the wild enthusiasm of the generous
Australian crowd, MacLaren and Peel galloped gaily to victory. Peel was due to pick up a third pair of spectacles, but
two were enough for this tour.

IV

England had to wait nine years for another victory on Australian soil. The winning captain was P. F. Warner and this
was my favourite tour, just as my favourite tour-book was
Warner's account of it called *How We Recovered the Ashes.*
It was my favourite, because it was my first, and I have
recounted elsewhere how, aged about nine, I bowled and
batted every ball of the 1903-04 Tests on the kitchen hearthrug. Victory was gained by three games to two; you might
say that the second (England) and the fifth (Australia) were
settled in advance by the luck of the toss, but the other three
went to the better side and on two occasions this was undoubtedly England.

If history were to award an order of merit in sheer quality
to Tests, the first game of this tour must stand very high, perhaps in the first two or three games of all games (always after
Jessop's match of 1902), certainly in the first half dozen. This
game had ' everything '; that is, everything that a thirst for
drama and excitement could reasonably demand. Winning
the toss on a batsman's dream of a pitch, Australia might
have been expected to pile up a colossal score; as it was, they
lost three wickets, including Trumper's, for 12. Noble then
took charge and though the phrase ' captain's innings ' is too
often used without meaning, it might well have described his
133, as bravely defiant a knock as any captain ever made.
Facing a total of 285 England started just as badly as their
opponents had done. Warner got a duck and Tom Hayward

failed, but Tyldesley played faultlessly and Arnold, sent in as pre-lunch watchman, defended with all his might. But the curtain rose on the most spectacular scene of the drama when Foster and Braund came together. By the end of the day they had taken the score to 243 for four. It was the next morning that the two of them showed the inhabitants of Sydney how bowling could be collared. Braund hit hard and often but Foster was positively dazzling, pouring out strokes from a cornucopia of plenty that only Trumper could have matched. When Braund was out for 102, there was a partial collapse, but, after that, Foster found two steady partners in Relf and Rhodes and with them actually put on 245 for the ninth and tenth wickets. Foster, who was last out for 287, had played what Warner has said was the finest innings he ever saw. In fiction we often read how fours flash from the bat; from R. E. Foster's they did.

You cannot make Australians feel that a position is anything worse than difficult. In the second innings Duff, Hill and Gregory all played well and Trumper batted superbly. It is the highest praise to say that he batted as finely as Foster had batted the day before and against even more hostile bowling. Old Australians will tell you that there has never been a tenser battle than that between Trumper and Rhodes. At the beginning of the last over of the day Trumper ruefully pleaded. ' Now, Wilfred, give us a bit of mercy.' And Rhodes shook his head. When stumps were drawn Trumper was 185 and Rhodes had bowled forty overs, taking five wickets for 94. Better batting and bowling have probably never been seen in the same innings.

Set 194 to win England, after something of a scramble, reached home safely by five wickets. The heroes of the game were Foster, Braund and Rhodes on the one side and Trumper on the other, but Warner has always believed that the match was truly won on the first morning when Hirst and Arnold took the first three wickets for 12.

It was almost impossible for the other Tests to stand comparison with the qualities of the first, yet there were one or two sensational happenings in the second. England had a chance to amass a good score on the first and second days, but a wet Sunday intervened and on Monday the wicket had become savage and brutal. The last three English wickets fell for 9 runs. Australia were in trouble from the first over and only another incredibly wonderful innings by Victor Trumper, first in and last out, saved them from the humiliation of a follow-on. In England's second innings there was also only one man, Tyldesley, who rode the storm, with 62 out of 103; but the wicket continued to be unspeakable and the first innings lead could not be overhauled. Australia made 111 (35 by Trumper) and England were two up. Rhodes took fifteen wickets for 124 and what his figures would have been if at least half a dozen catches had not been missed, nobody will ever know.

Australia won the third Test, mainly at the expense of poor English batting and the scene was now set for the possible decider. To some extent the result was influenced on the first day, not by the wicket, but by the solid batting of Albert Knight of Leicestershire who, as we shall see, was a man of deep religious conviction and played cricket, as Milton wrote poetry, ' as ever in the great Taskmaster's eye.' His batting was sturdy and strong and his 70 not out was worth its weight in devotional literature. The middle part of the game was supported by some fine bowling from Rhodes and Arnold and some steady batting from Hayward and Warner and then Australia were set 329 to win.

They believed, as Australians always do, that the task, if not easy, was quite possible. It was hostile bowling and eagle-eyed fielding which undid them. Hirst bowled McAlister with a bewildering swerver at 7 and Arnold struck a vital blow by having Trumper l.b.w. at 35. Bosanquet was put on, almost as a routine measure, a little while before tea and took two wickets in his first two overs. After that nobody could do anything with Bosanquet who at one time dismissed four baffled and bewildered batsmen for 12 runs. There was a dashing last-wicket stand between Noble and Cotter and 57 quick runs were put on to the delight of the Sydney crowd, and, for a short time, to the detriment of Bosanquet's analysis. Then Hirst bowled Cotter all over the place and England had won the game and the rubber by 157 runs.

On the day the rubber was won, C. B. Fry wrote to Warner : ' It is not the opportunities that count one way or the other. What counts is how they are used. You have used yours to the best advantage and you have won your campaign.'

V

The 1911-12 tour, also captained by P. F. Warner, marked the peak of the English ascendancy before the first world war. Some may claim that Warner's second side were most triumphant of all touring teams, though admirers of Chapman's 1928-29 side may dispute this. At any rate, there was a kind of Edwardian spaciousness about its composition and it rolled up the opposition in a truly imperial manner. It began unhappily, for Warner, after having scored 150-odd in the first game, fell a victim to the illness he has doggedly fought all his long life with a courage that once drew from George Hirst the spontaneous tribute : ' My, Mr. Warner, if you'd had a stomach like me or Schofield, you'd have been a Champion !' J. W. H. T. Douglas came in to act as his deputy and, though perhaps not immediately so happily genial in his leadership as Warner, he brought to battle the iron determination that was his own.

England lost the first Test, mainly because of their inability to play the bowling of H. V. Hordern, who, ironically, was a practitioner of the googly that Bosanquet had introduced eight years before, and of whom Sir Jack Hobbs has always spoken with wry respect.

The second Test started even more fantastically than the first of 1903-04. Then, you will remember, three Australian wickets fell for a dozen runs on a plumb pitch; now, in circumstances no less favourable to batting, they lost six for 38. The destroyer was Sidney Barnes, who at one moment had taken four for one and a little later five for six. From that point Australia staged a fighting recovery and England, despite a polished century by ' young Jack ' Hearne and a stubborn sixty by Rhodes, were only 80 in front. In Australia's second innings it was F. R. Foster's turn to wreak destruction, and England won by eight wickets, their total enriched by a beautiful not out century from Hobbs.

The third game at Adelaide uncannily repeated the pattern of the second. Australia won the toss and were rudely bundled out on a good wicket, mainly because they could not play the medium-fast bowling of Foster. England topped the 500 mark, with 187 by Hobbs and substantial scores by Foster and Rhodes. Australia, however, rallied strongly at their second attempt and England, instead of winning easily by an innings, were forced to bat again and lost three wickets in making the hundred-odd runs necessary.

The shape of things was firmly set and there was no altering them. In the fourth, and decisive game, Barnes once more shattered the Australian defence in the first innings and Douglas, who was a fine bowler in his own right, did the damage in the second. In between England piled up the gargantuan total of 589, starting with a first-wicket partnership of 323 which remained as an all-Tests record for 37 years. (When an England first-wicket stand reaches double figures nowadays, we think that things are looking up after all.) England won the last match of the series by 70 runs and so a side, powerfully armed at all points, brought home an overwhelming victory.

It was a victory of all-round dominance, in which Barnes, Foster and, at a later stage, Douglas, formed the armoured attack. Barnes and Foster did not so much defeat the enemy as bowl them out of existence. Batsmen found that the earlier googly bowlers could make a slow ball come quickly off the pitch; Foster and Barnes could make a fast ball come off even faster, and if this was an illusion it was an illusion that deceived batsmen of the quality of Trumper, Hill, Kelleway and Armstrong. The strength of the bowling was its greatest, but not its only, strength. The batting power was massive; Hobbs and Rhodes were an opening pair as impressive as the subsequent masters, Hobbs and Sutcliffe, and the bewildering run-stealing technique for which the second pair became world-famous was built up by the first pair. I remember once hearing Rhodes reveal the subtle secret of this semi-miraculous technique. ' I'll tell you,' he whispered in his hoarse, confidential voice. ' When I'm coming I say Yes and when I'm not I say No.'

Even if the unfortunate Australians could get either Hobbs or Rhodes out, there was the dazzling Woolley to come, and young Jack Hearne, who made a Test century before his twenty-first birthday, not to mention Frank Foster, whose batting was as dashing as his bowling.

And the fielding . . . A touring side has always a better chance of welding itself into a coherent fielding combination

D

than a side at home who only play together as a team
five times. But this 1911-12 side rose high above the standard of even the most agile touring teams. Hobbs, the quickest
cover point between Jessop and MacLean, would without
question have been worth his place even if he had been bottom
instead of top of the averages. It now seems scarcely credible,
considering our present acceptance of lowered fielding standards, but it is a fact that Hobbs ran out fifteen people during
the tour, while the number of runs he saved by his mere
intimidatory presence was enormous. And Hobbs was only
one of eleven in the field that included Woolley, who was
capable of taking half a dozen catches in a single Test, E. J.
Smith, who kept wicket like the Tiger that was his nick-
name, and eight more fielders who could catch or stop anything in sight or flight and could cover each other so perfectly
that there almost seemed to be twenty-two players in the field
instead of eleven. It is almost impossible to think of a side
as powerful, and yet . . .

VI

Maybe there was. In 1928-29 there went out a side, under
A. P. F. Chapman, which many critics consider England's
strongest touring combination. Perhaps they are right. It now
seems almost a blasphemy that Woolley should have been
left out, especially after his glorious 1928 season, but, otherwise, the team was about as strong as it could be.

'There have been teams,' says the contemporary *Wisden*
with its wonted sober judgment, 'which included players
more brilliant and more skilful individually, but rarely has a
side gone to Australia and played from beginning to end of
a strenuous and in many respects a tiring tour with the team
spirit so admirably maintained in every engagement.'

Ponder for a moment a Test batting order which ran:
*Hobbs, Sutcliffe, Hammond, D. R. Jardine, Hendren, A. P. F.
Chapman*, and then went on: *Larwood* (who made 70 in
the first Test), *Geary, Tate, Duckworth* and *J. C. White*. If
one of these needed a rest, there were batsmen like Mead,
Leyland, and Ernest Tyldesley; bowlers like Freeman, and a
batsman-wicket-keeper of the calibre of Ames, who, owing to
Duckworth's brilliance, never got a game in a Test. They

played twenty-four matches, of which they won ten, drew fifteen and lost only one. This was the fifth Test, after the Ashes
had been truly won and England had to take the field without
Sutcliffe and Chapman. Incidentally, this game was the frame-
work for the second Test century by a young man from a
hitherto inconspicuous spot called Bowral, which has now
been firmly planted on the map. Of the tourists' inconclusive
games, some were drawn owing to bad weather, but in others
the Englishmen were the victims of their own colossal scoring.

Their batting strength was gigantic. (Look at the names
again.) Their bowling was short in quantity and held no sharp
double-edged sword like Barnes and Foster. The weapons it
did include were (a) the fastest and (b) the best fast-medium
bowlers in the world at the time, with assistance at need of
(c) a slow bowler from Somerset who, it appeared, could bowl
practically all day and all night. As for the fielding, there
was nowhere a weak link in the chain. Hobbs was still Hobbs,
Hammond did in the slips what Woolley had done before
and, of the others, Chapman was only one of several continuously ready and willing to make 'impossible' catches.
Fielding skill is more difficult to assess and it presents few
formal figures for comparison as do batting and bowling, but
in any evaluation of fieldsman in this century, Chapman
could claim a place near the top.

The batting was almost arrogantly triumphant from the
first, and scores of the order of 406, 528, 486 and 734 for
seven were amassed in the early State games. When they
made their first score of under 300—it was 293—they won
by an innings. Not all their batsmen had a chance to play
in the big games, but Mead and Ernest Tyldesley frequently
hit up high totals in the lesser ones, and Leyland, coming in
for his injured fellow-Yorkshireman, Sutcliffe, in the fifth Test,
played like an old campaigner. A veteran warrior was Philip
Mead, who had been a member of the victorious pre-war
side, and he received with puzzled pleasure the greeting of a
Sydney Hill enthusiast : 'Whatcheer, Digger, I remember
your father in 1911 !'

In the first Test at Brisbane England were fortunate to
the point of embarrassment : first, in winning the toss, and
then in the luck they would have far rather not have had,
the illness of Kelleway and the injury to Jack Gregory, which

tragically put him out of cricket for ever. Hendren made 169
and Larwood took six for 32. Australia in their second innings
were practically atomised and White had the fantastic figures
of four for 7.

England's victory by 675 runs was in the realm of the
grotesque, but in the second Test at Sydney the dominance
was firm and clear. After a destructive spell of bowling by
George Geary (five for 35) England proceeded to pile up a
mammoth score. The master who ruled the whole series was
Hammond, and his was an imperial sway. In this game his
251 was a thing of beauty, starred by glittering off-side play,
and at the same time a feat of endurance. In the Australians'
second innings there was obstinate resistance from Woodfull and Hendry, but, though faced with a respectable score,
England won by eight wickets.

The third was the critical Test. It almost always is. The
struggle was a tense tug-of-war, with fortune swaying first this
way, then that. Australia, after a tremulous start, compiled
the excellent score of 397, which included two centuries and
a hard-hit 79 from that young man from Bowral who, though
no one knew it yet, was to be the hammer of the English
for the next twenty years. But he was not yet England's lord
and master. Once more Hammond was king and emperor,
off-driving majestically and ruling the bowlers with a rod of
iron. Jardine was his most fruitful partner. In the second
innings Australia again brought forth two centuries, one from
Woodfull and one from Bradman, the forerunner of so many.
England were asked to make 332 to win and though this
would not have been an insurmountable task in normal conditions, it was a different matter when the weather, and with
it the wicket, turned suddenly ugly.

History, they say, repeats itself, if only in the sense that
an indigestible cucumber repeats itself, unpleasantly and em-
barrassingly. Here was duplicated, with even greater intensity,
the titanic struggle that had been fought two years before at
the Oval. Then Hobbs and Sutcliffe, on a venomous wicket,
had defied the Australian attack for the best (and worst) part
of a day. At Melbourne, the same Hobbs and Sutcliffe scored
105 for the first wicket and if one of them had been out, the
rest of the side might have gone down like skittles. It was a
triumph of artistry, guts and footwork. While changing a

cracked bat Hobbs sent in a message advising his captain to put Jardine in next and when Jardine joined Sutcliffe, each defended in his own way with his own individual skill. The wicket was still viperish, but these two held on till close of play.

In the morning Jardine was soon out, but his departure was followed by two fine stands, first between Sutcliffe and Hammond and then between Sutcliffe and Hendren. That day Sutcliffe was monarch of all he surveyed. When I watched his innings at the Oval in 1926, I thought it about the most courageous effort I had ever seen on a cricket field, but Australian friends who saw the Melbourne match say that his 135 there was an even more magnificent achievement. At the Oval he was battered black and blue; at Melbourne his bruises were an abstract for a Turner sunset. Without offering anything but sympathy for the sore feet and fingers of 1955, I should like to take on tour a cine-film of Sutcliffe's bruises in glorious technicolor just to show how much an older generation could take. When Sutcliffe was out at last, 14 runs were still wanted. Chapman got out trying to knock the cover off the ball and Tate by 'backing up for everything,' but Geary settled the matter once and for all with a swashbuckling four and the rubber was won.

It therefore did not greatly matter that England won the fourth Test, after a ding-dong struggle, by 12 runs, in a game in which Hammond hit two centuries, scoring nearly 300 for once out; it did not even matter that they lost the last match, after another hundred from Bradman, by five wickets. At the end of the series the crowd gathered outside the pavilion at Melbourne, for all the world as if it had been Kennington Oval, calling for the players by name and yelling themselves hoarse. M. A. Noble, unsentimental warrior of forty-two Tests, observed of this scene: 'I cannot remember a similar happening in Australia. It was obvious that the Englishmen had left a splendid impression on the public mind as ambassadors of Empire . . .'

And again *Wisden* observed ungushingly: 'One may assert with confidence that few if any bodies of men have gone through a tour together with such splendid harmony prevailing all the time.' One who travelled with them said that he never heard a wry word. 'A happy family off the field, they pulled together in every match like a well-oiled machine.'

On the top of all their other qualities these men had perfect confidence in their captain and in themselves. Their imperturbability was rattled only once. That was when a Tasmanian umpire brilliantly caught Jardine at square leg.

VII

The 1932-33 tour was called the controversial tour and of this I will only say that the two Englishmen who were at the time reckoned (very wrongly, I think) to be the villains of the piece, are now regarded in Australia with as much respect and, indeed, affection as any native hero of the game. This fact, at least, must be counted to the credit of everybody concerned. In any event, during the tour any amount of good cricket was played by both sides that was not controversial at all.

The bowling of Larwood was, as we know, the greatest single factor in England's four-one victory, but it was by no means the only one. There was, for instance, Larwood's batting in the fifth game in which he made 98 by tremendous hitting. There was also the bowling of G. O. Allen who took twenty-one wickets in Tests without, in the general excitement, getting as much credit as he deserved. Furthermore, there was the flawlessly accurate bowling of Verity, whom even McCabe, the most aggressive of the Australian batsmen, could never knock off his length. Consistently fine batting form was shown by Sutcliffe and Hammond, each of whom scored exactly 440 runs in the Test series; there was a maiden Test century by the Nawab of Pataudi, slow but very sure; and there is the stirring story of Paynter who in the fourth Test rose from a hospital bed to play one of the most heroic innings ever played. It was a fitting reward that in the second innings he had the privilege of making the winning hit with a towering six.

An immense amount of fine cricket, too, was played by the other side. To suggest, as some writers did at the time, that this series was a mere matter of mayhem, is to belittle the exploits of many splendid Australian cricketers: of McCabe, a dashing cavalier incapable of an unsporting action, of the almost unbowlable Woodfull, of Fingleton, now one of the most fascinating of cricket writers, and O'Reilly, the authentic Tiger, who during this series bowled with as much devilish cunning as he ever employed, before or since. And the tour contained one major incident which deserves to be remembered as surely as one or two incidents deserve to be forgotten. In the second Test at Melbourne Bowes bowled Bradman first ball. I will repeat that :

D. G. Bradman, b Bowes   o

But if Bill Bowes was not the more surprised of the two I will be eternally astounded.

VIII

The latest side to visit Australia was highly successful, against all the omens, and England in the last two series has won both home and away. Look at this as sourly as you may, there is some credit here and something not inevitably calling for pessimism. Let us be mean. Let us be as censorious as if we were paid to be so. England won, but only because they were the less worse of two bad teams. If we humbly accept this, there is one small question to be asked : ' Why did our poor incompetent victims then go straight out to the West Indies and beat the living daylight out of teams featuring Worrell, Weekes, and Walcott?'

England, they say, were a four-man team. Let us consider this. I yield, as they say, to no man in my admiration for Tyson, Cowdrey, May, the best young batsman in the world, and the admirable Statham. But they were not alone. Behind the wicket was Godfrey Evans. I am sixty years old and I have seen most of the great cricketers of my time; it is impossible for me to reckon most batsmen today as good as Fry, Ranji, Jessop, Trumper or Hobbs or most bowlers today as good as Rhodes and Blythe, Barnes and F. R. Foster. But when I think of the great wicket-keepers I have seen—and I have seen them all, from David Hunter to Bertie Oldfield, not forgetting Lilley, who held the post for England against all comers and almost seemed as if he were going to reign as long as Queen Victoria—I have no doubt that Evans should have a rightful place at the head of any aristocratic company.

And there was Bailey. Whoever undervalues Bailey is scoffing at the principle that buildings need foundations. While Evans is in the line of the great wicket-keepers, Bailey is hardly in the line of the greatest all-rounders, like Hirst, Rhodes, Jackson, Noble and Armstrong; but that is not the point. What he has brought to the English sides of which' he has been a member is invaluable; he has provided them with the spinal support they have conspicuously lacked since the days of Maurice Leyland. At least three times in 1953 Bailey saved the day. His worth to the 1954-55 team was incalculable. There was not a Test game, even the ever-to-be-forgotten first one, in which he did not play a fighting part, either with bat or ball. A four-man team, indeed!

And do not forget Wardle, who will hit sixes when other men falter, or Appleyard, whose absence, perhaps more than any other, was sadly felt in the season of 1955. But the best reason for claiming that England was not merely a four-man team was the captaincy of Hutton, astute, tenacious, rich in experience, unperturbed by misfortune and above all endowed with patient wisdom. Indignation, especially in retrospect, is an enemy to the good life; but it is difficult to keep the blood at a low temperature while thinking of the ill-natured, ill-judged criticism which was sprayed on England's captain. But he kept steadily on his way, consolidating as he went.

In *Australia 55,* by far the best book on the tour, Alan Ross has said of Hutton that he is a civilised, adult and un-interfering captain. ' He deserved all the praise in the world for England's success: that one criticises him at all is because it would be insulting to judge such a great player by any but the highest standards . . .' The result, when it came, was brought about by spectacular bowling, some good batting and first-rate captaincy. That illness should have put Hutton out of cricket for a long period has been a tragedy both for a fine man and for English cricket. The one comfort in the unhappy event is that England's captain against South Africa was Hutton's vice-captain in Australia. In that position a young man of character and intelligence could, and did, learn much. A great man could not have wished for a worthier successor.

CHAPTER 5

SOME UNCLES AND NEPHEWS

I

THERE IS a certain fascination in considering the theory of re-incarnation, not to be confused with Pythagoras's other theorem about the squares on the sides of those regrettable right-angled triangles. The general idea is that the souls of the departed do not depart absolutely, but enter into a new tenancy in another body, moving on at intervals until they have received the full treatment. Thus, when the faithful are plagued by a stinging twanging mosquito they do not swat it ill-naturedly, as you or I might. The reason is humane and clear : it might be Aunt Agatha. Without pressing the theory too far, it is at least a pleasant fancy to wish that the soul of Jessop might just once enter into the scarcely sentient bodies of some of our county batsmen or that an England first-wicket pair might occasionally catch, however fleetingly, the spirit of Hobbs and Sutcliffe.

Without promising, like Sir Toby Belch, to draw three souls out of one weaver, we might at least scan the new generation for a new Hammond or a new Hendren. In one sense every human being is an individual, himself and no other.

In another and admittedly less important sense, he is, like Ulysses, a part of all that he has met or at any rate a part of all that has gone before him. There is always someone (or something) from whom, consciously or unconsciously, he appears to have derived his qualities. Thus, when Maurice Tate came, it seemed that he might be the new Barnes; when Alec Bedser came, he was possibly the new Tate. Who is to be the new Bedser I do not know; if he is to be half as good as the not very old one, he will have to be very good indeed. And it is impossible for an old Essex (or England) supporter to watch Trevor Bailey in resistant mood without thinking of the man who was surely his spiritual father: John William Henry Tyler Douglas.

II

The best phrase to describe J. W. H. T. Douglas is Browning's 'ever a fighter.' He was, of course, a boxer as well as a cricketer, winning the amateur middle-weight championship in 1908. His every act during a cricket match was an act of hostility and combat and his constant attitude was one of obstinacy and dogged endeavour. When Essex, or England, was in trouble, he instantly formed himself into a one-man resistance movement. In his own grim way he thought of England as something to rescue, something to get out of a hole. Whenever you saw him, batting with his back to the wall, or bowling to batsmen impregnably entrenched, you felt that that was the way he liked it; that a game was hardly worth the trouble unless you were fighting desperately to save it and that if the road did not wind uphill all the way, his journey was not really necessary. All his cricketing life was a struggle; in his first county game, as an eighteen-year-old Felsted schoolboy, he got a pair, twice clean bowled by George Hirst's swervers. It was characteristic of the man that throughout his county career he put up his best performances against Yorkshire and it does not need a couch-borne psychiatrist to explain to us that he was for ever afterwards 'taking it out of' Yorkshire for those two ducks.

As a bowler he was equally determined; he attacked the batsman with every ball. Even in the golden age that had as its ornaments such great fast-medium bowlers as Barnes and F. R. Foster he was noted for his 'bite' and breakback. He rose slowly to notice by sheer donkey work during the first decade of the century. He was, as we have seen, chosen as P. F. Warner's vice-captain of the 1911-12 Australian touring side and the stroke of ill-fate which laid P. F. Warner on his back set Douglas on his feet. A man of his stubborn character was bound to have what are charitably called the defects of his qualities. For one thing, he was far too conscious of the number of fools in the world to suffer them gladly in bulk. Warner, as always, was tact personified; Douglas was not.

It is one of the legends of the game that in the first Test,
the only one lost, Douglas put himself on with the new ball
and that Barnes said : ' That's all right, Mr. Douglas, but
what am I out here for?' These differences were soon cleared
up, mainly in what may be termed hospital consultations by
Warner's bedside, and everything that followed—the four
victories and the magnificent bowling of Barnes, Foster *and*
Douglas—was to the credit of all concerned.

Douglas's habit of ' keeping himself on too long ' was no
mere expression of egoism. He was tireless in his endeavours;
he simply could not believe that his attack would not eventually be rewarded. (W. G. Grace felt exactly the same.) The
apocryphal observations attributed to the wise-cracking Cecil
Parkin are tributes rather than criticisms.

' Very well, Mr. Douglas, thee bowl 'em in and I'll go on
after tea and bowl 'em out !'

' That's right, Mr. Douglas, thee go on at t'other end;
maybe tha'll see t'scoreboard better from there . . .'

Nothing could discourage him; nothing could distract his
attention from the three stumps twenty-two yards away; and
nobody, while he played for Essex, could give him as strong
a support as he felt he needed.

His temperament thrived on misfortune and had plenty of
adversity to thrive on. He did the ' double ' in 1914, the first
Essex player to perform the feat, and he was to do it four
times more, though there was no more cricket for five years.
In 1920-21 he led a hurriedly chosen side on a tour of Australia, one of the most disastrous tours in history—after all,
you cannot lose more than five Tests at a time—and yet, all
through the uphill fight, his intractably dogged qualities won
universal admiration. He had with him batsmen of the calibre
of Hobbs, Woolley, Hearne, Hendren, Russell and Makepeace, but somehow the very pertinacity of Douglas's batting
made it the most impressive of all.

The 1921 Tests in England were only slightly less cala-
mitous. Douglas was captain in the first two games and both
were lost. Here was a captain who had lost seven Tests in a
row. Was this a record? For the last three games Lionel
Tennyson took his place as captain and in these Douglas, in
spite of, or even because of his displacement, played with his
usual courage and tenacity. Altogether he played in twenty-

five Tests, and there was not one which he did not make a personal battle.

He battled on as captain of his county until 1928 and then, owing to temperamental differences with the committee, he was obliged to resign. This was a personal tragedy for him, a tragedy genuinely comparable to W.G.'s break with Gloucestershire thirty years before. And by a greater tragedy two years later he lost his life by drowning. He had been visiting Helsinki with his father on a business trip and their ship on her return voyage was in collision with another in a Baltic fog. When last seen, he was struggling to rescue his father as the ship heeled over. He died a gallant gentleman and a stubborn Englishman.

III

Trevor Bailey, who is now secretary of the Essex county club, as a small boy attended the preparatory school kept by the late D. R. Wilcox, Cambridge batsman and Essex captain. In later life they collaborated in an excellent instructional work, *How to Train Young Cricketers*. From prep school Bailey went on to Dulwich, a school noted for first-class cricketers, including F. H. Gillingham and S. C. Griffith, Hugh Bartlett, D. R. Wilcox, and a gaggle of Gilligans. He was captain of the Eleven in 1942 and, along with his friend A. W. H. Mallett, was reckoned among the outstanding schoolboy cricketers of his time. But then he was an outstanding games player, adding a talent for Rugby football and athletics to his other accomplishments. His last year at Dulwich, when he was captain, saw him play in a large number of fine wartime games at Lord's.

He went straight from school into the Army, or rather the Navy, joining the Royal Marines and leaving after the war as a commissioned officer. He played a few games for Essex in 1946, the year of his demobilisation, and in 1947 he went up to Cambridge, gained his blue as a freshman, and hit 60 in his second innings in the Varsity match. During the following years he happily shared his seasons between Cambridge and Essex and his enthusiasm plus his skill with both bat and ball made him a valuable member of both these sides. He was selected for his first Test in 1949 against

the New Zealanders and from that time on it was difficult
to think of an English side *sans* Bailey.

Since then, up till the end of 1955, he has played in thirty-
two Tests : six against New Zealand; seven against the West
Indies; three against Pakistan, seven against South Africa
and nine against Australia, and has made three tours, one
to the West Indies and two to Australia. His virtues are con-
spicuous : he is a fastish bowler who can hit the stumps;
a fielder with safe hands and a swift return, and a batsman
who can be as stubborn as Johnny Douglas ever was. While
the Australians called Douglas, Johnny Won't Hit Today, they
never found a suitable name for Bailey (except Barnacle)
though they might well have claimed that Trevor Won't Even
Hit Tomorrow. His stubborn front has never been a popular
front with enemy fielding sides and sometimes he has suffered
from critics who should know better and from spectators
who know nothing at all.

From the time when he first won a place in an England
side he has been its sheet anchor. Some of his critics have
claimed that he was more sheet than anchor, but this is
demonstrably untrue. Anchor he has undoubtedly been. In his
first series against New Zealand in 1949 his batting and
bowling were both outstanding; in 1950 injury kept him out
of all but two of the games against the West Indies but he
did finely in both of these. F. R. Brown's 1950-51 tour of
Australia marked a watershed in Test history, for though
Australia won four-one, one small turn of Fortune's wheel
might easily have made the result three-two the other way.
While a broken thumb kept him out of the third and fourth
Tests, he played a hero's part in the first and second; in the
first, that crazy Brisbane game in which England declared at
68 for seven and Australia at 32 for seven, Bailey took three
for 28 and four for 22; in the second Test, another frenzied
game, he took four for 40 and two for 47. His first appearance after breaking his thumb brought him a century and the
first Test in New Zealand brought him another. Well might
his opponents cry : ' Bite you your thumb at us, sir?'

In 1951 he suffered further injuries, but in spite of torn
fibres in his back he made 93 in the fourth Test against the
South Africans at Leeds. He was not chosen to play against
India in 1952, but the year after in the vital recovery rubber

he was the victorious side's most valuable member. Not every man can be directly a match-winner, but in a long exhausting series in which most of the games are unfinished, one man may often be a match-saver. The match-winners in the only finished Test of 1953 may well have been Lock and Laker, but in the four drawn games there were several match-savers. Alec Bedser certainly saved, almost won, the first; Watson, with one other, saved the second; Wardle saved the third; Laker and one other saved the fourth; and in the fifth there was, as I have said, fine bowling by Lock and Laker, not to mention some grand tear-away stuff by Trueman, but the true turning-point of the game was Bailey's dour, dogged innings of 64. If he had failed, England could hardly have survived. Several players saved their side once; Bailey saved his side at least three times. He was the real cricketer of the year.

In the half-disastrous, half-triumphant tour of the West Indies, Bailey again made a supreme effort to provide England's batting with the backbone that it sadly lacked. Sometimes it seemed that when Hutton was out, everybody was out. In the fourth and fifth Tests he went in first with his captain and in the last game, which England won so that they were able to draw the rubber after being two down, he 'went mad' and, in a feat of bowling rare in any kind of match, took seven for 34 on a batsman's wicket. It was the climax of a splendid individual tour and if nobody wrote an admiring calypso about it, a great opportunity was missed.

In 1955 again he performed prodigies of stubborn resistance against the South African visitors. Some critics thought him too dour and for the last match he was dropped. Wild horses would not make me abuse selectors, but it is conceivable that they could have been mistaken in this decision. As matters fell out, Tyson became unfit and Bailey was called in, after all. The way in which he was cheered all the way to the wicket must have been positively embarrassing to him. He did not do well with the bat in this game and was not called on to bowl a great deal. Nevertheless my own feeling is that Bailey should play for England as long as backbones are needed. That will be for a long time yet.

I have meant to paint Trevor Bailey as a man of iron

courage, but I have not told you all. I once heard him give a
lecture and, to the awed astonishment of all present, he by-
passed the customary 'Mr. Chairman and gentlemen,' and
burst incontinently into song. He did this, starting from cold.
It was an act of heroic hardihood.

IV

Not long ago, I had the infernal cheek to send a copy of
a book of mine to a distinguished author who has written
beautifully about cricket and almost everything else. 'Your
picture of cricket's Golden Age is incomplete,' he said. 'I
grant you your Hirst, Rhodes and Jackson, but, because you
are an incurable Yorkshireman, you have forgotten some of
the other counties and you have neglected the young batsman
who was the golden figure of the Golden Age. I mean K. L.
Hutchings . . .'

Some cricketers mature late, some mature early, and some
mature very early indeed. These are the darlings of the gods.
K. L. Hutchings was not the most renowned of all Kent
cricketers. That crown must, I think, rest upon the brows
of Frank Woolley. But after Woolley, who? Towards the
end of the first decade of this century, Kent dominated the
kingdom of cricket as imperiously as Yorkshire had ruled it
at the beginning. They were powerful at all points, with such
bowlers as Fielder, Fairservice and Colin Blythe, all-rounders
like J. R. Mason and the unparalleled Woolley, and batsmen
like C. J. Burnup, Seymour and Humphreys. But the most
dashing and dynamic player of this great Kentish age was
Kenneth Lotherington Hutchings, who when he first played
for the county had not left Tonbridge school.

At Tonbridge he remains a legend and is reckoned, despite
competition with F. H. Knott, L. P. Hedges and one other,
the most remarkable batsman to have played in any school
eleven. He was born at Southborough in 1882, the youngest of
four brothers. All the brothers were valiant members of the
school side. Kenneth was in the Eleven for five years, from
1898 to 1902, captaining it in the last two. In 1902 he scored
a thousand runs, a rare feat in any short school season, and
in one game made 205, a record score for the school. Those
who played with him then described him as 'a terrifying

master of bowling.' It was said not merely that he punished bowlers but that he *basted* them.

In the year after leaving school he was again invited to play for Kent and in much less than a full season he had an average of nearly thirty. Even as early as this an England captain was saying that, if this boy Hutchings could play regularly, nothing could keep him out of an England eleven.

Nothing startling occurred in the next two years, but in 1906 all those who saw him play fell under his spell and those who missed the privilege wondered what it was that had so bewitched their friends. This was Hayward's year, when the batsman who had first partnered Bobby Abel and then Hobbs scored an aggregate of over 3,500 runs, which remained a record for over forty years until both Compton and Edrich knocked the bottom out of it in 1947. Yet, such is the power of personality that the sensation of the year seemed to be not honest Tom but a young gentleman from Kent.

While in county matches Hutchings scored 1,358 runs with an average of well over 60, it was not the number of his runs that enchanted the spectators, but his magical manner of making them. This was a black season for Yorkshire, for by a blow reminiscent in its deadliness of Greek tragedy, my county lost the championship by one run. I can remember to this day little knots of men deploring the disaster in Leeds City Square and hushed voices.

But once the first pain of the amputation was over Yorkshiremen did not grudge Kent their photo-finish triumph and they remembered the dashing batsman who had lent an additional glow and gleam to the wing of Kent's victory. *Wisden* named him one of the five cricketers of the year and, throwing its usual cautious outlook to the winds, asserted roundly: 'There has not been so remarkable and individual a player, since Trumper and Ranjitsinhji first delighted the cricket world . . .'

His was an attacking genius; his batting was the sword-play of a D'Artagnan. From nobody's bat—or certainly from nobody's bat but Jessop's—did the ball hit the boundary rail with such a short, sharp shock. Like the very greatest of batsmen, he appeared to have plenty of time to play his stroke, even off the very fastest bowling; he seemed to hit the ball, and hit it ferociously hard, at the last fraction of a second. What was more, he was no erratic genius, but was as consistent as he was coruscating. He would play back for defence and forward for attack and his style was all his own. It was said that Trumper had at least three strokes for every ball; nobody knew how many strokes Hutchings had, but he seemed never at a loss. He could occasionally be beaten, but never tamed. In earlier years his pulls were daring and sometimes disastrous; there never were such strokes for breaking bowlers' hearts and fielders' fingers. As his style grew more mature, though no less individual, he pulled less and drove more. The result was even more devastating. Even George Hirst, the finest mid-off who ever lived, was known to move back a yard or two.

Hutchings went to Australia with A. O. Jones's 1907-08 side, but on the whole did not do himself justice. No more did anyone else, on that somewhat luckless tour, but in the second Test at Melbourne—the only game that England won—he hit up a glittering century, including a six and twenty-five fours. It was the only Test innings of the true Hutchings vintage. His health was not at its best and he suffered especially because his individual attacking style required that he should be permanently in the pink of condition. In the Oval Test of 1909 he scored a dazzling 59 and it was sad that there were no Tests in 1910, for then he could do no wrong and seemed on top of the world. His most striking quality was his inspired and inspiring confidence which, when he was physically fit, was perfect and absolute. A friend of mine in that year saw him one sunny morning cycling down to the Tunbridge Wells ground to play against Lancashire. 'Hullo,' called Hutchings. 'I'm going to get a century today.' In point of fact, he got a century and twenty runs more.

Like many another gallant cricketer he gave his life for his country in the 1914-18 war. Good players are many; great players are few. Players with the touch of sheer magic—a Ranji, a Trumper, a Kenneth Hutchings—are fewer still.

V

In 1946, the first year after the war that the public schools came back to Lord's, I saw a boy of thirteen play for Tonbridge against Clifton, probably the youngest ever to play at headquarters. No doubt the contemporary Tavern cat and even some of the sparrows in front of the Members' and Friends' stand were his authentic seniors at the time. I have seen many a Test at Lord's but never a more gripping battle than that game. An elderly gentleman who learned his cricket in Yorkshire is not apt to gush over an encounter between two south country schools. But facts are facts.

This thirteen-year-old, who batted in the key position of No. 3 on a sticky pitch—Tonbridge had been put in—made 75 and this was more than all the rest of the side put together could muster. They were led on the first innings by over 50 and, when they went in a second time, they were even less successful; this time, while our hero made but 44, only two others made more than 10. Clifton were set a mere 118 to get for victory and they would undoubtedly have got them, but for the bowling of this same astounding boy. Tonbridge won in the exciting end by two runs and this would never have happened if he had not taken five wickets for 59. His name is Michael Colin Cowdrey and now, though he is still only twenty-three, he is an England veteran.

Wisden said of him at the age of thirteen that he was a natural stylist and has had no reason to change this view. Not all his school appearances at Lord's were so like a Boy's Own Paper serial story as his first, though, even in the matches which Tonbridge lost, he never failed to take wickets or make a reasonable score. In his last Tonbridge v. Clifton game he took seven wickets, missed a century by as few as three runs and nursed his school to victory in another palpitating finish after they had only just escaped the follow-on. In that year he made over a thousand runs and took fifty wickets, played for Kent while still at school and captained the Lord's Schools against the Rest. A darling of the gods, indeed.

Some schoolboy rockets come down like the stick but this one has remained a fixed star in the sky. Cowdrey has been as impressive a member of the Oxford and Kent sides as he had been at Tonbridge. In 1952 he made a century against the touring Indians; in 1953 he made four centuries, one of them in the Varsity match, and, an achievement of far more moment than any of the others, a couple of masterly fifties against the Australians.

It is easier to assert that a player is of the highest class than to explain what is meant by the phrase, but Cowdrey's accomplishments adorn their own tale and to watch him make fifty is to see an innings stamped as surely with quality as is old silver. If you were to come suddenly upon a game in which the name of the sturdy young batsman at the wicket was unknown to you, you might well rub your eyes.

' But surely,' you would murmur, ' that's Walter Hammond . . .' You would be wrong, but the momentary illusion would be striking: the poise, the set of the sturdy shoulders, the deceptively lazy swing, the power and majesty of the off-drive, and, above all, the complete mastery of the difficult situation, would all be there. All these were the imperial prerogative of Hammond; all of them appear to be budding in Cowdrey.

He was only twenty-one when he first played for England in November, 1954, on that stricken field of Woolloongabba and, by all accounts, he was the best sight for English eyes that day, a genuine gleam in the gloom. Coming in when three wickets including Hutton's and May's, had fallen for a song, Cowdrey had to decide upon his own strategy. His partner, Edrich, went at 25, but then he was joined by Bailey, an old hand at the Gibraltar game. The two of them put on eighty of the hardest-won runs England ever made. For Cowdrey it was a baptism of fire, with Lindwall and Miller as the leading fire-raisers. He made only 40 but every run was worth its weight in plutonium. Whatever happened in that nightmare game, England had found at least one badly needed new batsman. That was his first Test and it needed no great gift of prophecy to say that he would play in many, many more.

So this amazing tour went on; up from the depths of Brisbane the Englishmen struggled desperately back. In the second innings of that memorable second game at Sydney, May made his own kind of splendid century and Cowdrey stood by him in an invaluable partnership of 116. It was the most palpitating game of the tour and its heroes were two young batsmen and two young bowlers. In the third game at Melbourne Cowdrey stood almost alone, except as almost always, for Bailey; here was his first Test century, 102 out of 160 put on while he was at the wicket. His confidence, coolness and concentration were those of a man who had made many Test centuries. May came back, as he invariably does, with an invaluable second innings and, after Tyson's almost incredible bowling spell of seven for 27, England were one up. The fourth game was a further triumph for England and once more Cowdrey played a big part, with 79 runs, which were all splendidly made.

The 1955 season was for Cowdrey a long story of illness or injury, with banes on his fingers and blights on his toes. Nevertheless, the quality is there and will remain, and no misfortune, minor but maddening, has succeeded in marring Cowdrey's confidence. I do not know if every morning, like Hutchings, his spiritual ancestor in confidence, he says: 'I am going to get a century today.' Whether he says that or not, he will make many centuries. He will enjoy making them and you will enjoy watching him.

I have a disagreeable friend who thinks cricket a dull game and cricketers a lot of boring young fellows with one-track minds if any. But he will go out of his way to make an exception of Cowdrey.

'Now there's an intelligent young feller,' he said, 'interested in a dozen things besides cricket . . .'

Coming from where it did, it is a sincere tribute.

VI

The bowler has in his armoury two major weapons: cunning and ferocity. As Yorkshire was divinely appointed from old time to be the spiritual home of left-hand slow bowlers, so Lancashire has often bred and always striven to nurture the men of speed and fury. There was Crossland, there was Mold (born in Oxfordshire), there was Macdonald, the Australian with the beautiful action, and now there is Brian Statham, whom people even outside Lancashire regard as something of a paragon. Chronologically in the middle of this devastating dynasty came Walter Brearley, the most highly coloured character of them all.

Brearley, who played his first county game against Sussex in 1902, became a regular member of Lancashire in 1903 and for the next ten years or so, with time off for injuries and disputes, he lived and breathed and had his exuberant being in the midst of a conflict which, in the poet's phrase, was not without dust and heat. As Schofield Haigh was the sunshine of the Yorkshire eleven, so Walter Brearley was Lancashire's thunder and lightning. He loved bowling as Mrs. Battle loved whist and Mr. Jorrocks loved hunting. He was a stickler for the rigour of the game and when you faced him, you faced the image of war, no doubt without its guilt but with considerably more than twenty-five per cent of its danger. Oh, but he was a tearaway, let-me-get-at-him, put-me-on-at-the-other-end, bang-goes-his-middle-peg kind of a bowler and on a fiery pitch his fiery spirit was in its element.

In 1904 he took twelve for 144 in his first Old Trafford game and throughout a year in which Lancashire were worthy county champions, he was the head and front of their attack. At the end of this highly successful season he was unaccountably left out of the Lancashire side in the game which the champion county played against the Rest. At this he exploded, resigned from the county club, consigned its committee to the utmost depths of Tophet, gave up the blasted game for ever, and was back in the team the following May, bowling away with happy fury. That was Walter all over. He was a supremely lovable person, but to be lovable is not necessarily to be amenable. From the beginning to end he was a thorn in the flesh of authority, but no doubt he thought it served authority right for being so fleshy. The ' good boys ' have their virtues (I am a good boy myself) but fast bowlers and, say, paratroopers, whose first duty is sheer violence, have their virtues, too, and it is asking much to demand that a character who is at his best when hurling thunderbolts should at all other moments of existence behave like a pale young curate.

For Brearley, 1905 was the first of his three great years. He flung himself into the battle like a projectile and right through the season he kept up the pace as if he hated the law that forbids a bowler to bowl at both ends. In all he slew 181 victims, 131 of them on his county's behalf. His slightly miraculous match was against Somerset at Old Trafford. In this he took seventeen wickets, four of them in four balls, for just over eight runs apiece.

He also played for England against Australia under Jackson's invincible leadership and took fourteen Test wickets for no more than 20 each. He was as near to being Trumper's bugbear as any bowler who ever lived. That ought to have been enough to satisfy any one man's ambition.

Without any reason the Gloucestershire match at Old Trafford turned itself into a battle royal. It began with a joke. Now Walter loved a joke, but he preferred to make it himself. Someone spoke with less than respect of Walter's batting. It was as though someone in a Victorian cavalry mess had spoken lightly of a woman's name and before either side knew what was happening the Gloucestershire batsmen found themselves suddenly subjected to a bombardment compared with which the alleged ' bodyline ' of twenty-eight years later was mere soft-ball stuff : Walter was not meek. But facing him was a man, Gilbert Laird Jessop, who was not meek either. The faster Brearley bowled, the harder Jessop hit; it was a battle of gods and titans with forked lightning flashing across the sky. Batting at the other end was Jack Board, a stumper with scarred hands and a stout heart and he was content to defend himself, but Jessop took the war into the enemy camp, hooking Brearley's jet-propelled full-tosses time after time over the square-leg boundary. Spectators held their breath. Somebody was going to get killed. Fortunately, before that happened, Brearley bowled both batsmen and, after that, Lancashire won rather easily. But relations between the counties were strained for a long time. And all because somebody had suggested that Brearley was perhaps not so classic a batsman as MacLaren or Spooner.

In the next two years he attended to business and played very little cricket, but on the few occasions on which he played he showed himself the most destructive fast bowler in England. In 1907 he could play no county cricket but he came in for the Gentleman v. Players game and took ten wickets in the two innings. In 1908 he came back to Old Trafford, kissed and made friends all round, flung himself into the county fray with his old demoniac fury and performed so admirably as to be granted *Wisden's* order of merit as one of the five cricketers of the year. It was not claimed that he had the sheer pace of Kortright or the grandeur of Tom Richardson, but the critics lauded his spirit of aggression, his untamably dynamic force and his inexhaustible energy. In 1909 he had another remarkable year, taking 115 wickets for just over 15 runs each; 1910 was, owing to injury, almost a blank and in the sunny summer of 1911 he turned out less than a dozen times. Whatever the dispute with his county may have been, 1912 found him playing for Cheshire, and not so destructively as might have been expected in the minor counties competition.

It was only natural that Brearley should strike his highest note in the annual Roses battle. He never bowled except to hit the wickets and it was a far greater joy to him to hit a Yorkshireman's middle stump than anyone else's. In the famous Sheffield game of 1905, which Uncle Walter took me to see, Brearley took thirteen wickets, while I prayed heaven to visit him with the fate of Dathan, Korah and Abiram. He incredibly took twenty-five wickets in the two games of 1908, both of which Lancashire lost, and altogether in fourteen Roses matches his bag was 125. Yorkshire's batsmen agreed that he was a holy terror, but all agreed even more fervently that a Roses match would not have been the same without him. Once at Bramall Lane he was barracked for a vociferous succession of l.b.w. appeals. The ball that finally bowled the batsman broke the middle stump and Brearley seized the fragments, dashed across to the Grinders' Stand and addressed his 20,000 critics : ' All right, then, how was *that* ?'

After the war he appeared again in that astonishing game in which A. C. MacLaren's team of youngsters (plus a veteran or two) conquered the hitherto unconquerable Australians of 1921. In that game Brearley hurt himself, jumping over the pavilion rails. (He was always jumping over pavilion rails, because in his impatience to get to the wicket he could not be bothered to open the gate. He was the only fast bowler to run out to bat nearly as fast as he ran up to the wicket). After the game his captain thanked him warmly. ' But why thank me, Archie ?' he demanded. ' After that little accident I could hardly play and you know I couldn't bowl at all.'

' True,' said MacLaren. ' That's why we won.' Those two were prize kidders long before the days of Sergeant Flagg and Sergeant Quirt.

Walter Brearley was a turbulent spirit, irascible, magnificently self-opinionated but when all was said and done, truly lovable. We ne'er shall look upon his like again.

VII

The contrast between Walter Brearley and Lancashire's (and England's) most consistent fast bowler of today is almost that between a 'wicked' old uncle and a 'good' young nephew. It is a difference in techniques, but even more it is a difference in generations. I have often asked: can the fast bowler, a man born to violence as the sparks fly upwards, be at the same time a model citizen? The answer, at least at the present time, is: yes. If it were possible to discover on the cricket field, or anywhere else, a quieter, more modest young fellow than Frank Tyson, it would be Brian Statham. It has always seemed to me a small miracle, forming part of the larger miracle of England's 1954-55 triumph in Australia, that its four youthful heroes were all well-mannered, thoughtful, rather diffident and self-effacing young men. May, Cowdrey, Tyson, Statham—it gives the heart a lift to picture them: the best of contemporary youth. They have courage, steadfastness and high technical skill. In his triumphs Tyson displayed neither the exuberance of a Miller nor the relentlessness of a Lindwall; he just bowled very fast, very accurately and got them out. Statham bowled nearly as fast, often a little more accurately and took any of the wickets that Tyson left standing. As a pair they had long spells of irresistibility so that each Australian batsman must have felt like a body with Burke waiting for him at one cemetery gate and Hare at the other.

In the following summer Tyson had one devastating Test against the Springboks and then injury either kept him out or quelled his powers. In the second Test Statham bowled supremely. It was the game of his life so far. His performance was not a sudden streak of lightning; it was a feat of controlled and sustained brilliance. The South Africans, as they afterwards proved, were a fine batting side, but at Lord's Statham destroyed them. His figures were seven for 39 and they did not in any way flatter him. He bowled 29 overs, of which twelve were maidens, and bite and precision were in almost every ball.

This twenty-six-year-old Manchester lad began by preferring tennis to cricket and graduated to his county from club and Royal Air Force games. His N.C.O., more impressed by his bowling figures than Brian himself had ever been, asked for a trial for him at Lord's. The authorities there, noting his place of birth, did what no Government department would ever have done, used their deductive powers and suggested Old Trafford. When he obtained a forty-eight hour pass for the purpose of visiting that delightful spot, it rained for forty-eight hours.

He went to Old Trafford as a spectator the next year—it was 1949—and, sitting behind the arm of the sorely tried Dick Pollard, saw at any rate that life for a fast bowler was not all beer and skittles. This was the first county match he had ever seen: the following year he was playing in one. George Tribe, Northamptonshire's astute Australian, saw him playing in a club game. Wheels began to turn and the invitation to visit Old Trafford was repeated. A fortnight after he had reported to that shrewd old coach, Harry Makepeace, he was given a chance to play against Kent. There is a story that, for his first match, he came along with his cricket boots in a brown paper parcel. If that is true I will swear that the parcel was neat and tidy. The first blood he drew in county cricket was that of the prolific first-wicket batsman, Arthur Fagg. Not bad for a brown paper parcel. In his first Lancashire v. Yorkshire match he twice fell flat on his face on the greasy pitch as he ran up to bowl. But in the same eventful over he hit the middle stump with a beautiful breakback and his victim was Frank Lowson, a highly valued scalp for a tenderfoot's belt.

He was not given a full county season but he bowled well enough to take 37 wickets and to receive an S.O.S. to fly out, with his team-mate Roy Tattersall, to reinforce F. R. Brown's casualty-stricken side in Australia. Since this visit his bowling figures have been remarkable for their consistency:

1951	...	97 wickets at		15.11
1952	...	110	,, ,,	18.08
1953	...	101	,, ,,	16.33
1954	...	92	,, ,,	14.13
1955	...	101	,, ,,	14.25

Besides his unbroken county service and his Australian trips, Statham played in a Test against the South African visitors of 1951, toured India in 1951-52, where he gained a reputation for hitting sixes, and by his steadiness played a more than worthy part in England's drawing of the rubber in the West Indies in 1953-54. Hutton's determination to launch what amounted to a twin-engine bomber attack was not so successful in the West Indies as it turned out to be a year later in Australia, but all the time Statham was the bowler who never wavered. Up to the end of 1955 he had played in twenty-five tests.

His action, with its smoothly accelerating seventeen-pace run, is formidable, but not ferocious, his powerful left shoulder pointing at the batsman and his body pivoting from the hips as the ball flies from the hand. He bowls ' tight ' and, like the old-fashioned fast bowlers, he attacks the stumps directly. He bats left-handed, occasionally with effective violence, and, wherever he finds himself when not bowling, he generally looks the surest and most agile fielder in sight.

Modesty nowadays in public figures is often no more than an empty convention, a cliché to furnish forth the caption. In Brian Statham it is sincere and genuine, as is shown by the way in which he has been willing to watch and learn from more experienced attackers, such as Bedser and Lindwall. Whatever he has learnt, he has learnt with intelligence and imagination. If anyone thinks it odd that a very fast bowler should have a noticeably even temper, Statham will tell you that when a bowler loses control of his temper he loses control of length and direction as well. His good temper is matched and supported by his droll humour. A friend of his (and mine) once told me that, at the end of a successful M.C.C. tour, they were bidding a rather sentimental *au revoir* until the English season opened.

' Well, so long,' said Brian. ' It'll be nice seeing you up at Old Trafford. I'll give you a dolly one to get off the mark. And then, by gow,' he added in tones of pure friendship, ' I'll pin your ears to t'bloomin' sight screen.'

CHAPTER 6

CAPTAINS COURAGEOUS

I

ALL COUNTY captains are courageous. If they were not, they would not take on and sustain so onerous a job. If ever captaincy was a sinecure, it is not so now. Some, like Marlar of Sussex, come to it as young amateurs; others, like Perks, who retired from the captaincy of Worcestershire at the end of the 1955 season, attain the post as senior professionals. Amateur or professional, they have many responsibilities and few privileges. Yet they do their job, all seventeen of them, and with high competence. Their problems and their materials vary immensely and each one of them in his own way does work that is individually praiseworthy. If your side finishes the season at the bottom of the table, it does not necessarily mean that you are a bad captain. If, on the other hand, your side stays at or near the top, season after season, you may be excused for suspecting privately that you are moderately good.

II

Captain Forceful

That stout-hearted Lancastrian, Leonard Green, led his county to the top three times in a row in the exciting years of 1926-28 and, after that, he retired from a captaincy which had been one hundred per cent victorious. Yorkshire, under Brian Sellers, won the championship seven seasons out of nine. But no captain except Stuart Surridge has gone on skippering a conquering side in his first four successive years. Surrey won in 1952, 1953, in dank and sombre 1954 and in sub-tropical 1955. The weather was all one to Surrey and to Surridge.

What kind of fellow is this architect of victory in quadruplicate? First, a big man, both in body and spirit. To the bulk of an amiable buffalo he adds the agility of a jaguar. (I once heard an admirer at the Oval say of his slip-catches : 'He don't catch 'em; he eats 'em!') He is a big man; was a big boy, and, I imagine, must have been a big baby. At anyrate he was playing at school at the age of eight. His family have been for three generations manufacturers of cricket bats and almost every other type of sports equipment. In winter he works hard at this expanding business, besides giving an eye to two farms, where grow the willows which the family firm shape into bats. He progressed in his burly, bustling way through the various grades of cricket at his school, Emmanuel, which is an excellent cricketing school anyway. First he was in the under-fourteens, then the colts, then in the first eleven, which he captained in his last year at school, when he was seventeen.

It is typical of Stuart Surridge that until he was fifteen he was a wicketkeeper. Why? 'They wanted a wicketkeeper.' You may have seen him at slip or short-leg suddenly (literally and laterally) hurl his fourteen-and-a-half stone, taking a somersault and a flying ball at the same instant. Maybe he was born with this jet-propelled jump; maybe he learned it keeping wicket. Then in his last couple of school seasons he became a fast bowler. ('Oh, well, they wanted a fast bowler . . .').

He was born a volunteer for energetic jobs. I can well imagine him modestly receiving a medal for gallantry and murmuring : 'Oh, well, they *wanted* a chap for stopping runaway trams . . .' He became a schoolboy member of the Surrey club when he was twelve and that put him in a position to see something worth watching : an eleven captained by P. G. H. Fender, and headed in the batting order by Sir Jack Hobbs and Andrew Sandham, the most serious rivals in their period to Yorkshire's Holmes and Sutcliffe. And young Surridge did something better than watching : he became a a pupil at the Easter classes at the Oval. These were looked after by that cheerful Surrey stalwart, Alan Peach, who has never received sufficient praise for his sterling all-round work as batsman, bowler, fieldsman and coach. Surridge learned a great deal from Peach and in the winter went on learning a great more from the school run by Sandham and Alf Gover.

The coaching he received from Gover was of the utmost value to the budding attacker, for Gover was one of the biggest-hearted fast bowlers that Surrey, or any other county, ever had. His record, which was striking, would have been much more so if he had had better support from the slip-fielders of his period. There is a tale (no doubt apocryphal) which pictures Gover having a drink with his fellow players after a particularly unhappy afternoon of sins in the slips. ' Well, so long, Alf,' said one of the leading offenders. ' I've got a train to catch.' ' So long,' said Gover cheerfully. ' Hope you have better luck . . . with the train.' Under Gover's tuition Surridge's bowling action greatly improved and was already on its way to becoming the bustling business-like affair that it is today.

Before he left school he was asked to turn out for the Young Surrey Players under the leadership of Alan Peach and it is a pleasant thought that in the same eleven were Arthur McIntyre, the county's present wicketkeeper, Bernard Constable, one of Surrey's regular batsmen in their four championships, and Alec Bedser, most famous Surrey bowler of modern times. There must have been a formidable quantity of talent running around in a team containing youngsters of that quality.

Surridge had his first game with the county second eleven in 1937 but it was another ten years before he reached the first team. He then played only five times, but the following year (1948) saw him turning out oftener and beginning seriously to take wickets. In this season he had good matches against both Warwick and Notts, and he performed so successfully that he was presented with his county cap. In the next three years he continued to advance by leaps and bounds, and those who have watched him bowling and fielding know that the leaps and bounds are physical and spectacular.

In 1952 he was appointed captain of the county team and it was no coincidence that Surrey had the best season they had had for nearly forty years. Actually they had tied with Lancashire at the top of the table two years earlier but they had not won the championship outright since 1914 when Hobbs batted and ' Razor ' Smith bowled them to victory. The *Wisden* of the time had no doubt whatever about the main cause of the county's win in 1952. ' One reason for Surrey's tremendous advance was the confident assurance of all the players in their own abilities, and for that happy frame of mind they had to thank Surridge . . .' He believed in attacking all along the line and going all out for twelve championship points from the first ball sent down. Time and again in that exciting season Surrey would knock off the runs in the fourth innings on a dusty wicket. Boldness was their friend, and they added to their obvious skill a courage and a confidence that pulled them through. Typical of this kind of game was the one against Kent at the Oval, when Surrey were set 190 to win in 92 minutes. With an hour to go, they still needed 128, and wickets kept falling. Each batsman hurried to the crease and when Surridge made the winning hit—it *would* be Surridge—the clock's minute hand was dickering on half past six and the Oval crowd were on their feet and yelling their heads off.

In that season, too, Surridge set up a Surrey record by taking fifty-eight catches in a season. I can think offhand of only one player, other than a wicketkeeper, who has done better than that. That was John Langridge in the year of his retirement. In the four championship seasons Surridge has held nearly two hundred and from what I have seen, he has ' made' a large number of them, which would not have been catches at all to a less acrobatic fieldsman.

In 1953 the county record was not quite so good, only thirteen victories being won instead of twenty, and early in 1954, that wettest of seasons, Surrey were robbed of win after win by the malicious caprice of the weather. Up to a point reasonably beyond the peril of overhauling, Yorkshire were well ahead and then, nine games from the end of the season, Surrey flung themselves into a terrific spurt. Yorkshire, in a most un-Yorkshire-like manner, wavered before the challenge, and Surrey ran out with eight wins out of those last nine games—bang, bang, bang, bang, bang, bang, bang, BANG.

The season of 1955 was as hot and arid as 1954 had been cold and soaking, but those who alleged that Surrey would be ' found out' by a long dry spell had to eat their words. Surrey attained their objective in spite of all handicaps: injuries, Test calls on vital players, initial collapses and Surridge's own woefully inefficient tossing. Like Hutton, the

captain who led English cricket back out of the wilderness,
Surridge is a chronically bad guesser as between heads and
tails. Surrey tackled their opponents as a terrier tackles its
victim : a grip and a shake, and all is over. In many ways
Surrey's triumph of 1955 was the most meritorious of all. In
the four championships 110 matches were played, 70 were
won and only 14 were lost. There is a chance, especially during a wet season, that a side may be robbed by rain of
almost certain victory. Surrey followed the soundest policy
for preventing this robbery by winning a big proportion of
their games in two days.

Apart from the inestimable gift of leadership, Surridge has
made a genuine contribution as a player. He is a battering
fast bowler who could no doubt have taken many more
wickets if Lock, Laker, Alec Bedser and Loader had not taken
them first. As a batsman he is a vigorous No. 9 with a good
eye and a strong arm. He can be a stubborn defender at need
and is by no means a mere thumper. In 1954 at Hove I saw
him hit two skimming sixes which rose like swallows straight
over the bowler's head and looked as if they would finish in
the English Channel. His fielding is a joy to the spectator
and a terror to the batsman and the praise so deservedly
lavished on the 1955 Springboks could as justly have been
given to Surridge's Surrey. To Surrey's superbly inimical
close-wicket fielding Surridge has contributed more than his
individual brilliance. Off the first ball he bowled in first class
cricket an easy catch was missed in the slips. Everyone
laughed. Without registering any rash oaths, Surridge made
a mental note that sloppy fielding was no laughing matter.
When he became captain the evil practice ceased. By precept
and example, but chiefly example, an almost infallible
machine of destruction has been built up. If catches were
now dropped close to the wicket, it would be a matter, not
for merry laughter, but for a short, sharp commination service.

Asked how a succession of four glorious championship victories had been brought about, Surridge answered in two
words : team spirit. Of course it was team spirit, but if anyone
thinks that the splendid thing called team spirit can come into
being without vital and inspired leadership, then he does not
know Surrey or Surridge.

III

Captain Friendly

In these years of Surrey's ascendancy, their closest rivals, except in the slightly hideous season of 1953, have been Yorkshire and Surridge's friendliest rival has been Norman Yardley. When Yardley retired at the end of the 1955 season many more people than Yorkshiremen were sorry. Seldom has one cricketer been so wholeheartedly liked in so many parts of the Commonwealth. It is one of the most difficult things in the world to describe a genuinely charming person and some-times a biographer will call a man charming because he can-not think of anything else to call him. There is something faintly derogatory about the adjective. Not so with Yardley. Here you have a naturally pleasant and friendly person, whose unfailing good temper does not deprive him of shrewd-ness and whose amiability shows anything but weakness of character.

Yardley's early career reads like a school story of the good old romantic sort. At St. Peter's, York, he was in the eleven for five years, two of them as captain. In his fourth year his batting average was just under 90, a colossal figure for school cricket. This gained him an invitation to play for the Young Amateurs against the Young Professionals at Lord's where he scored nearly 200 and made the interesting acquaintance of a young fellow called Compton (D.). Soon afterwards he received the call to the Yorkshire schoolboys' heaven, *i.e.* the nets at Headingley, where he came under the eye of George Hirst, the wisest and most fatherly of coaches, and the next year he made a century for the Public Schools against the Army, the first schoolboy ever to get a hundred in this match.

His cricket career at Cambridge had some of the elements of a royal progress. Winning a Blue in his first year, he scored 90 in his second Varsity match and a century that won high praise in his third. In 1938 he was Cambridge captain and was noted, like Kipling's fisherman, as a captain of infinite resource and sagacity. The previous winter he had visited India with an unofficial side led by Lord Tennyson; in the last English winter before the second world war he toured South Africa with the M.C.C. and wrote an amusing book about it. He had already been playing successfully for York-shire for part of three seasons.

The war saw him in the renowned Yorkshire regiment, the Green Howards, and he served with distinction in the Sicily landings and the bitter Italian campaign in which the gallant Hedley Verity received his mortal wound. Yardley was wounded, too, though, happily, not seriously. After the war he played for Yorkshire two seasons under Brian Sellers's cap-taincy; 1946 was the last year in which they won the cham-pionship outright, though they have shared it once and come in second almost monotonously. The immediate post-war period was a difficult time for both Yorkshire and England and there were no easy victories. Yardley was vice-captain to Walter Hammond on the M.C.C's 1946-47 Australian tour; England had on the whole a disastrous time, at any rate in Test matches, but this was certainly not the fault of Yardley who specialised in (a) stubborn middle-wicket stands with different partners and (b) getting Bradman out.

In 1947 he successfully captained England against South Africa and batted and bowled well enough to be named as one of Wisden's cricketers of the year. The following year saw the crushing invasion by Bradman's 1948 conquerors, for-midably armed at all points, and Yardley captained a not very strong England side against them with courageous ill-success. Responsibility curbed his naturally light-hearted approach, but it never made him grim and it certainly did not freeze the genial current of his soul. Early in that season he had a patch, as all good cricketers have, when he could do little right. In the Middlesex match my daughter and I saw him coming out to bat at twenty past one as the potential third party in a hat-trick. We crossed our fingers for him under our score cards and sighed audibly with relief when he returned to the pavilion for lunch, having survived a couple of as harrowing overs as I have ever watched in my life. After lunch he came back and scored 90, hammering the efforts of seven bowlers to all parts of St. John's Wood. And all the time he was suffering horribly from lumbago.

His batting is firm, his strokes are clear-cut and, unlike some modern batsmen, he is quick on his feet. In 1955, the year of his retirement, he was batting almost as well as he had ever done. In the field he has a sure pair of hands in any

F

position. I saw him run out one of the leading West Indies batsmen in the Lord's Test in 1950. It was a jet-propelled return that took the batsman's bails and breath away at the same time. Yardley's rather curious bowling action has been described as ' an inspired twiddle,' but it is far more effective than it might appear to the spectator—ask Bradman—and if he had only put himself on more, he would have taken many more wickets. But then he is a supremely gifted player of all ball-games and could probably have played baseball and American (or Australian) football just as well as he plays cricket, hockey, fives and squash.

Though a friendly soul, Yardley has some forthright ideas on the way in which the world of cricket should be run. He would cut the duration of Test matches from thirty hours to twenty-four (reckoning specifically in hours, not days); he would like, as would many thoughtful cricketers, to restore the old l.b.w. rule, at the same time compensating the bowler by ensuring that pitches were faster; and he would abolish the great gulf fixed between amateurs and professionals by paying those now called amateurs (who have to earn their bread the same as anybody else) the same amount as Australian cricketers are normally paid : a fixed match fee as compensation for time spent away from their work. This revolutionary but realistic policy might well keep in the game some of the vivider, lighter-hearted cricketers who will inevitably be lost to it.

In captaining Yorkshire and England, Yardley seldom enjoyed the best of luck, but I will wager he has enjoyed his cricket just the same. Yorkshire, home of the great allrounders, has in modern times produced very, very few better all-rounders and certainly never any player who, on or off the field, so richly fulfilled the definition of the Good Companion.

IV

Captain Purposeful

To me the question of amateur or professional captains is not a vexed question. It is hardly a question at all; other things being equal, I should have preferred an amateur captain, if only because, in the old days at least, he would have had fewer worries, but 'other things' are not equal and immense social and economic changes have ensured that they never will be. It is fruitless to peer at the question in the abstract, for the facts of life are concrete. Captaincy should go, not to the most amiable amateur or the most respected of elderly professionals, but to the best man for the job, and the operative word is *man*. My own feeling is that the right thing was done both when the national captaincy went to Hutton (though it might have gone with less apparent reluctance) and when it subsequently went to Peter May. In each instance the best available man for the job was chosen. This principle was undoubtedly followed when the Warwickshire captaincy went to H. E. Dollery.

I sometimes think *Wisden* might find it convenient to give a list of cricketers who were *not* born at Reading. Dollery would not find a place in this list for, like Peter May, Ken Barrington and a number of other eminent players, he was born in Reading. Dollery's home was near the county ground, whose custodian had a son playing for Warwickshire, and Warwick was the county towards which his thoughts, as a boy, naturally turned.

At school he was something of a schoolboy prodigy and performed feats more appropriate to a Boy's Own Paper serial than to the factual pages of *Wisden*. In his school's match against the M.C.C. in 1931 he made 101 out of 140 and in the same game in 1932 he carried his bat through the innings for 104. (The total score was 115 and his most prolific partner made three). If any story-writer allowed his hero to do that, he would be blackballed by every editor in Fleet Street. While Dollery was qualifying for Warwickshire, he turned out for Berkshire, making a double century against Monmouthshire, and was chosen for the Minor Counties side that played the West Indies touring side at Lord's.

In his first game for Warwickshire—it was against Yorkshire at Scarborough in 1934—he only avoided a pair by one run, but nobody worried about it. This was the extraordinary game in which Warwickshire, after having been skittled for 45, won a breath-taking match by one wicket, mainly through the muscular ministrations (twelve fours and three sixes) of the Rev. J. H. Parsons. Parsons' pleasure, indeed! The newcomer's inauspicious start was hardly noticed.

The following year Dollery gained his regular place in the county side and ever since has made his thousand runs every season, mostly when most needed. In 1955 he only just missed being the first batsman to reach them. What is more creditable still, he has always made them attractively. In 1948 he shared the county captaincy with R. H. Maudsley and in 1949 became full captain. In his first year as captain Warwick came fourth in the championship; in 1950 they were fourth again and in 1951 they climbed deservedly in to first place, for the second time in forty years. To this happy success Dollery made three major contributions: attractive batting, first-class fielding and genuine leadership, not from a lofty eminence but from the ground floor.

He was, and always has been, up till his retirement at the end of the 1955 season, a leader of determination and, as much as any county captain, has been the sworn foe of purposeless draws. From the first ball of every match it was his firm determination that the game should be finished and finished in Warwickshire's favour. In this aim he was abetted by ten other players who, under some infectious compulsion, shared his belief that Warwickshire were going to win, anyway. Like all good cricketers, he dislikes the repetition of the phrase 'brighter cricket,' preferring the more intelligent phrase, 'more purposeful cricket.' Most emphatically he dislikes the kind of modern game which doodles along in the doldrums and then, if lucky, ends in a tip-and-run scurry on the third afternoon.

He would not alter cricket as a game, but he would like to see a compulsory declaration at six o'clock on the first day, so that batsmen will not go to sleep after tea. His admiration is for batsmen who play the ball rather than let the ball play them and he has little respect for those whose technical equipment consists mainly of a gentle push-stroke in the direction of the fieldsman at short-leg. His own batting was always the reverse of this. In the Gentleman v. Players match of 1950 he showed his purposefulness by scoring an extremely attractive century. It was not his fault that the game ended in a draw, but he had a good deal to do with the fact that this was about the most exciting draw I ever saw. So long as there are captains who follow Dollery, with his technical skill and his tactical mastery, cricket will never be a dull game. There are certain arguments against a professional county captain. The best argument in favour is Horace Edgar Dollery.

V

Captain Urbane

Charles H. Palmer must be the most amiable gentleman who ever hurled a bombshell. In the last few cricket seasons this slender, gentle-mannered former schoolmaster has flung three. His first was a splendid fighting innings of 85 for Worcestershire against Bradman's all-conquering Australians of 1948 in which he treated the bowling of Lindwall, Miller, Toshack and McCool with a disrespect which even Hutton and Compton did not outdo at any time during the season. His second bombshell was thrown when, after being appointed secretary-captain of Leicestershire in 1950, he led his new county in 1953 to the third place in the table, the highest position ever attained by a side which had contained such all-time stalwarts as C. J. B. Wood, who once made two not-out hundreds in one game against Yorkshire, J. H. King who also made two hundreds in a Gentlemen v. Players match to which he had been invited as a reserve, Ewart Astill, who did the double eight times, and George Geary, one of the most genuine all-rounders and enthusiastic coaches who ever stepped on green turf. For three exciting days in August, 1953, Leicestershire actually held first place and, although the vision eventually faded, it did not fade very far.

Palmer's third bombshell was his feat in taking eight wickets for seven runs in May, 1955, against the champion county. At one time his figures were eight for nought and might conceivably, if unbelievably, have been nine for nought, and thus enshrined in *Wisden*, for ever and ever, world without end, *amen*. Everyone knows that Laker holds a record of eight for two, taken on a horrid wicket in the 1950 Test trial, and he went out to defend it with his life. His first ball he hit skywards and ran. Fortunately for Laker—lucky Jim!—it fell to earth, he knew not where, avoiding several clutching hands, and Palmer's analysis was dragged down to a mere eight for seven. Some people will spoil anything.

Leicester's 1953 season was not a tale of easy victories but of hard fighting, good batting, good bowling, good fielding and good teamwork. In the practice of these virtues Palmer played a more than adequate part. His batting is graceful in the style of the old masters and far more powerful than you would expect from such a slightly-built figure; his bowling is accurate, teasing and sometimes destructive; like himself, it has a pleasant air of innocence; his fielding is keen and safe; and the contribution of his leadership to a fine team spirit has been immense, in its enthusiasm, its intelligence and a certain dash for which opponents have been occasionally unprepared. In 1954 there were heavy setbacks but the following year Leicester were in the fight again and, after one or two storming finishes, they ran out a highly creditable fifth.

Palmer visited South Africa with George Mann's team in 1948-49 and was manager of Hutton's team in the West Indies in 1953-54. On both these occasions he did what he was called upon to perform, both as player and manager, with a certain distinction. And it requires no two-way stretch of the imagination to recognise that managing a West Indies tour is not all bananas and cream.

Four times in 1955 I went up to Lord's to see him and, if possible, have a word with him. The first time was in the Gentleman v. Players match and I saw him compile a century of academic flawlessness. On the other side his fair-haired team-mate, Maurice Tompkin, one of the best hard-wicket batsmen in the country, hit a century, too, that was easy on the eye. In the Middlesex v. Leicester game my time was limited; the moment I put my head in at the gate, I saw that Charles Palmer was bowling and he bowled all the time I was there; the second day he was batting all the time and batting extremely well. The third day he was bowling again and I had to go back to work without seeing him to speak to. I also missed the exciting finish of the game which Leicester lost, but lost honourably, going down with flying colours in an attempt to force a last-minute victory.

Here is a captain with a team of triers; a man of high talent and exceeding, even excessive, modesty. On the occasion when he had finished off the Surrey innings by taking eight for seven, he went round to his opponents' dressing-room. His expression was apologetic and his tone deprecating. What he said was: ' Sorry, chaps! *I only went on to let my other bowlers change ends!*'

VI

Captain Resourceful

Glamorgan's captain might have had a greater reputation as a cricketer if his reputation as a Rugby footballer had not been quite so great. The name of Wilfred Wooller stands so high in Welsh rugger history that it is at home among the very great: Gwyn Nicholls, R. T. Gabe, Wilfred Wooller. His qualities as a footballer were force, speed, and a kind of vivid resourcefulness.

As a cricketer his talents have been of a similar kind. He has gone for his objective as he used to go for the line a few years before. When Glamorgan won the county championship in 1948, it was their first victory since they became a first-class county after the first war. They did not owe this victory to their batting strength, which was hardly formidable, but to some fine bowling and splendid team fielding.

Glamorgan was a 'welded' team. It had its own Welsh inspiration and possessed a particular form of unruffled concentration induced by gay and skilful leadership. It was mischievously whispered that Glamorgan gained rather than lost by the comparative modesty of their batting strength (though this suggests no disrespect to W. E. Jones and Emrys Davies) because the very moderateness of the scores they made gave their bowlers plenty of time to get the enemy out for less. Indeed, Wilfred Wooller was heard to say, no doubt with a wink, that there were even better bowling sides in the country. Whatever Wooller said, however, there were few better fielding sides, and there was hardly a single fieldsman as brilliant as Wooller himself unless it was that remarkable all-rounder, Alan Watkins.

Wooller began his education at the famous Welsh school, Rydal. From there he went up to Cambridge and first played cricket for Glamorgan in 1938 without setting Swansea Bay on fire. But before the war, in which he had the unpleasant experience of being a prisoner of war in Japanese hands, he flung himself into Glamorgan cricket with all the enthusiasm he had previously called up to hurl himself over the enemy line for a winning try. In 1947 he took over the captaincy and in 1948 he led his men to triumph. Since then the county has seen ups and downs but in 1954 at least they rose from tenth to fourth place. And among the sides they defeated were Surrey, the champions.

A strong, forcing right-hand bat, he had for a long time the habit of placing himself, with excessive modesty, at No. 7 or even No. 8, but halfway through 1954 he gave himself a well-deserved promotion to No. 1, and he showed his appreciation of this promotion by performing the double for the first time at the age of forty-one. When in true batting form, as he frequently was during the 1954 season, he would go down the pitch in the old-fashioned way and drive gloriously over the bowler's head. He has played many times for the Gentlemen and has well deserved the honour.

One of his secrets, apart from pure enthusiasm, is the way in which he has helped to knit eleven individuals into a streamlined fielding side, of which every player is an integral part and everyone knows, even if he does not bowl and has made a duck, that he has a chance to have a good number of runs and to applaud his team mates for doing the same thing.

Wooller is a master of cricket strategy and part of this strategy is to make certain that his men participate in the tactics of the game. Cricket, he has said, is a game ' requiring thought and brains ' and to such purpose has he used his thought and brains that, according to a pretty legend, other county captains are apt to feel a little innocent in his hands.

But that, of course, is only Wooller's Welsh fervour and his Welsh fun. I once heard a humorous complaint from Jack Cheetham, the 1955 Springbok captain. There was only one thing, he said, more embarrassing than walking slowly down the ninety-two steps of the pavilion at St. Helen's, Swansea, to the tune of *Sospan Fach*; and that was walking slowly *up* the ninety-two steps of the pavilion at St. Helen's, Swansea, after you had got a duck. It also illustrates the form of dominance exercised over the innocent visitor by Wilfred Wooller's Glamorgan.

VII

Captain Eager

E. D. R. Eagar has been captain of Hampshire since 1946 and so has been a county captain longer than any of the present holders of the office. Yet though he may be named the *doyen* of captains, not one of them is more alert in the field or fuller of energy at the end of a hard day. He was born in Cheltenham and made his début with Gloucestershire while still at Cheltenham College. He played in several games for the Oxford eleven in 1938, but did not gain a Blue, which is a little ironical, seeing that, when playing for Gloucestershire against the Varsity, he hit up 82 in quick time. After the 1939 season he was, like the rest of us, deprived of cricket for too long a time, but when the war was over, Hampshire appointed him captain-secretary.

Hants did not do so well in his first year, but at least they beat Yorkshire, the champions, and though they appeared a moderate fielding side, Eagar himself was a notable exception. The next year the story was similar: a poor season, but Eagar fielded like an angel of light, taking 34 catches, most of them at short leg. The year 1948 brought all-round betterment; the county rose from sixteenth in the table to ninth. Hants were the only side to gain a first innings lead over Bradman's all-conquering Australians; and again Eagar gained the praise bestowed by sober *Wisden* on the man who was willing to go all out for victory. And so it has gone on.

Hampshire have had their ups and down; 1949 and 1950 were down and 1951 was an up in which as many as eight young players had better figures in either batting or bowling. After that there were three lean years, which saw some good individual performances but no degree of cohesive success. And then came the wonderful season of 1955 in which they climbed to third place, a higher position than they had ever reached before.

The bowling was not merely painstaking; it was varied and effective, for the older fastish men became more penetrative than they had ever been before and Peter Sainsbury, in his first full season, showed himself a leg-spinner who may well be called to higher things. So keen was the attack that only one individual century was scored against it. The fielding reached a level higher than its usual high standard and the batting seemed to improve out of all knowledge. Though reckoned less important than bowling and fielding, it may be said of batting, as was said by a famous peer of church attendance, that there is no positive harm in it, and while

Hampshire batting improved greatly, the individual style and exuberance of Roy Marshall, their West Indian all-rounder, has been a constant joy.

As for Eagar himself, the most frequent praise bestowed on him is that he gets the best out of his men, and after 1955 he must for the first time have been nearly satisfied. He has seen his reward for years of enthusiasm, encouragement and sheer hard work. But sheer hard work to him is a greater pleasure than it is to most people and he is the sort of man who, after a gruelling day in the field, would challenge the nearest fieldsman to a race to the far boundary. His energy is inexhaustible and his cheerfulness is as wide as his smile. Of all the Desmonds in the worlds here is one who will never be called Dismal, for he has led Hampshire to the highest pinnacle of her history.

VIII

Captain Kyd

If I were young enough and a good enough cricketer I should be proud to serve under any of the captains we have glanced at; if, without the entanglement of local patriotism, I might choose a captain playing today for an ideal county side, I should choose Stuart Surridge; but if I were allowed to pick a captain of yesterday, I would go back to the decade before the second world war and call up the leader whom Yorkshire folk regard as the true embodiment of their county in action. Yorkshireness as a quality, has existed in all cricket's ages : always it is a fighting spirit, as in Emmott Robinson, or Arthur Mitchell or Fred Trueman; sometimes it is a *cheerful* fighting spirit, as in Tom Emmett, George Ulyett, George Hirst or Johnny Wardle; the good fight is eternally fought. In the nineteen-thirties the fight was crowned by a series of victories, almost, but not quite, unbroken and the leader in this long triumphant campaign was Brian Sellers.

For the best part of thirty years before the first world war Lord Hawke presided over the county's destinies in a leadership stamped with the high autocratic tradition. His was a firm but essentially benevolent autocracy and there was not a Yorkshire professional who was not grateful to him. With that war many things were lost for ever, some bad, some

M. C. COWDREY
At twenty-three, an England veteran

MR. AND MRS. NORMAN YARDLEY
with two singles and a two

CHARLES MACARTNEY
'They call him the Governor-General
because he's so cocky'

W. S. SURRIDGE
'A big man, both in body and spirit'

WILLIE WATSON

'In the old-fashioned phrase, a gentleman in word and deed'

R. A. McLEAN

'Dazzlers are precious because they are rare and grow rarer'

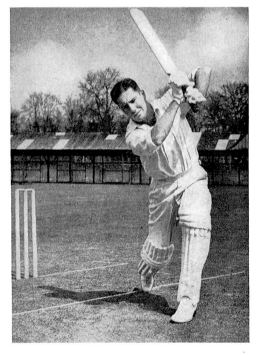

Top left:
GEORGE HIRST
'The one I loved the best . . .'

Top right:
S. M. J. ('SAMMY') WOODS
'Fire, fury and fun . . .'

Left:
LORD HAWKE
'An untiring worker to improve the status and rewards of the cricket pro . . .'

NEIL HARVEY
'Started with beautiful strokes from the first ball he received'

BRIAN STATHAM
'I'll pin thi ears to t'sightscreen . . .'

FRED TITMUS
'Steadiness, persistence and a technical skill much higher than it looks . . .'

TREVOR BAILEY
'Should play as long as England needs
a backbone'

CHARLES PALMER
'Captain Urbane . . .'

GEORGE COX
'Integrity, intelligence and extreme likeability'

FRANK WORRELL

'Meandering lazily to a fifty while fast-scoring batsmen make ten'

SIR DONALD BRADMAN & A. B. SELLERS

'Sellers . . . a symbol of the will to win only surpassed by Grace and Bradman'

good. No one wants to lament the bad and it is just as fruitless to lament the irrecoverable good. Both are gone for ever. In the years immediately after the war the Yorkshire side was a mighty and formidable entity. It would be wrong to say it did not need captaining, but, like a massive mechanism, it did not need driving, only starting and steering. Of the several Yorkshire captains between Lord Hawke and Brian Sellers, all were gentlemen and players of merit, though not of equal merit, and it can be said without disrespect to any of them that Sellers, during the nineteen-thirties, was an outstanding leader.

Sellers came to the captaincy after the first half-dozen matches of 1932, when that dashing bat and daring close field, Frank Greenwood, was obliged to resign for family and business reasons, and at once he made his mark, not spectacularly but steadily. He was the son of Arthur Sellers, a notable opening batsman of the eighteen-nineties, and he took steps to improve his batting but, from first beginnings, he had something else to bring that was of greater moment than sound batsmanship, important as that may be. Force of character is easy to recognise, but hard to describe. On the silver screen it may be portrayed by glaring eyes, corrugated brows and a voice like the bark of a neurotic bulldog. Anybody who has ever met true force of character knows what a ludicrous travesty that is, for force may go with a quiet voice and good manners.

Cricket is a game, but in Yorkshire they follow the scriptural injunction: whatsoever thy hand findeth to do, do it with all thy might. You naturally keep the laws and play fair, but within the game's written and unwritten rules, you strain every nerve to win. If you are the sort of person who couldn't care less whether you win or not, you are poor in spirit, but undeserving of any beautitude. You are paying your honourable opponents a poor compliment if you cannot be bothered to beat them. Without the will to win on both sides no game would be worth while. Sellers was a solid symbol of that will to win to a degree only surpassed (and I would not take two great names in vain) by Grace and Bradman.

Coming into what was an almost terrifyingly powerful eleven, he first took pains to make himself a capable member of it. Every day, at the wicket or on the field, he was learn-

ing something. Soon he had turned into a more competent
No. 6 batsman and passed the ordeal by intimidation with
honours to qualify as a first-class 'suicide' fielder. By the
end of his second season the Yorkshire committee were thanking him for his 'splendid example set in the field.' This was
something considerably more than a perfunctory compliment
to success. They do not very much go in for compliments in
Yorkshire, anyhow.

Since the turn of the century, Yorkshire had been a fine
fielding side. Gone was the slap-happy period of the early
nineties. In the first decade of the twentieth century Hirst was
the finest mid-off, while Tunnicliffe vied with Braund and
Denton with Johnny Tyldesley as the greatest slip and the
greatest long-field, in the world. Who is the finest mid-off
in the world today? I wish I could think of more than two or
three batsmen whose off-drive is hard enough and frequent
enough to care. The most brilliant fieldsmen of today—Lock,
Surridge, Milton, Watkins—are all 'hip-pocket' men.

Tight as was Yorkshire's fielding in the first decade, in the
third the grip became even tighter. Some of Yorkshire's young
captains of the period, notably Alan Barber and Frank Greenwood, were gallant close fielders; with them fielding was a
fine art. In the thirties Sellers carried the business one step
further: from a fine art to a form of psychological warfare,
legitimate but loaded with menace. It was, as the fieldsmen
might have explained, perfectly easy. 'All right, lad, if you
want to shift us, you *shift* us!' But Sellers and his associates
were seldom shiftable.

Leading his side out to field, Sellers somehow gave the
impression of the buccaneer captain leading his cut-throats
aboard the captive brig. Perhaps it was his walk or his expression of cheerful determination, but that is how he always
looked to me. His pirate mate was Arthur (Ticker) Mitchell
and the other villain was Cyril Turner, a particularly friendly
soul, who never snatched an 'impossible' catch off the bat's
edge, except in the way of kindness. The effect of this lower-
ing, threatening vigilance was that opponents coming out to
attempt a quite moderate fourth innings total were bundled
out for scores woefully below their reasonable hopes. A hypnotic influence was in the air. It was as though an invisible
choir were ceaselessly chanting: 'You'll never get 'em, you'll

never get 'em . . .' When Verity bowled on a wicket that gave him the slightest help, the ball would fly, as though under magnetic compulsion, towards Mitchell, who seemed to have as many arms as a Hindu deity. The batsman was virtually like Lazarus, bound hand and foot with grave-clothes.

In the eight pre-war years when Sellers captained Yorkshire he led them six times to championship victory. In 1946, the extremely difficult season after the war, he stayed on and led them to one more, which made seven out of nine. In the whole period Yorkshire played 258 championship matches and won 154. Only twenty-four games were lost. These figures, unlike most, are worth remembering. He had a magnificent side to lead : Sutcliffe, Leyland, Mitchell, Barber, and a young lad named Hutton; as bowlers, Bowes, Macaulay, Smailes and the incomparable Hedley Verity. But no one can deny that it was magnificently led.

People have said that Brian Sellers was hard. Of course he was hard. So are diamonds. Also like Sellers, they are rare. Of all the captains of all the counties in this or any recent period, and there have been many admirable ones, none has ever matched Brian Sellers for force, for fire, and for the refusal to accept dominance from anybody on earth. For me he will always be the friendly buccaneer, the pirate who weathered the storm.

CHAPTER 7

YORKSHIRE AT THE OVAL

I

THE LAST time I went to a county match at the Oval
Yorkshire were fielding. While I was paying my two shillings at the gate, Appleyard, whose subtle variation in pace
was a *rubato* movement in itself, was taking his third wicket.
The ground was crowded with excited Surrey supporters and
by the time I had woven my anxious way round to one of the
only available seats in the Vauxhall stand two further wickets
had fallen. I ardently wished success for my own county
but I felt, irritably and illogically, that they should not whip
the enemy so fast that their most faithful follower could not
catch up with the fall of wickets. When Surrey were out,
Yorkshire fared little better. It was sad to see Hutton go so
early. At that time few had realised that he was a sick man.
A duck by Hutton is no ordinary duck; it is disproportionately
a triumph for the other side and a disaster for his own.

The eternal debate between bat and ball continued. Every
run scored by either side had to be extracted like a back
tooth. Something of the joy of battle was in every ball and
it was a battle fought hand to hand and foot to foot. If there
was anything more heartening to the north-counrymen present than the bowling of Appleyard that day it was the batting of Watson, cool, trim and elegant. The day's play quivered
with excitement like a Roses match of the old days : no quar-
ter was asked or given : the bowling was merciless in its pace
or cunning and the fielding as tight as a fiddle string. Surrey
are the best fielding side in the country and that day Yorkshire were their equals. Watson, who had batted so admirably, was out trying to knock the cover off what looked like
the only loose ball I saw sent down.

Honest work is the root of all evil. Like most working
citizens, I normally see only one day of a match, and I had

94

to rely on the B.B.C. and the newspapers for the unwelcome information that on the third day Yorkshire, fighting every step of the way, had been beaten by 41 runs. Nevertheless, I confess that I have not for years seen a more enthralling encounter. The return game, which Yorkshire won by the skin of their teeth, must have been even better.

The background to the Oval, which has been described as ' unfashionable, unlovely and industrial,' has changed a good deal since I first saw it before the first world war. Unfashionable it may be, industrial it must be, but unlovely it can never be while the spirit of Jack Hobbs hovers over its great wrought iron gates. It was then as Cockney as Lord's was cosmopolitan. Lord's is still cosmopolitan, supra-national and slightly global; the Oval is still Cockney, though not so Cockney as it was forty years ago. I have heard inhabitants of more socially favoured regions describe spectators at the Oval as ' just like a Soccer crowd, you know,' but they have a sound knowledge and a high appreciation of the game. I remember a comment from a neighbour during the Yorkshire match a year or two ago. Trueman, who was doing his national service, had been released from the R.A.F. to play in this and the spectators were awed by the length of his run.

' National service?' growled my neighbour. ' Six overs o' that and he's done his national service!'

Like Yorkshiremen, frequenters of the Oval are unashamedly partisan. They do not assume the doubtful attitude known as objectivity, which means in fact that you couldn't care less; they frankly express the wish that Surrey will win. This is a sentiment which Yorkshiremen understand, appreciate and repudiate. Consequently I have seldom felt at more than the normal patriotic odds with any neighbours I may meet at the Oval. True, I often meet bunches of exiled Yorkshiremen at the Oval, where they are fewer but perhaps more vocal than at Lord's. Such interchanges of courtesies are all to the good, unless they go too far.

The Oval in 1914 was a less comfortable place than it is now. For the general amelioration Hitler and the Surrey committee are responsible, though not in direct collaboration. In the first place, Hitler's war caused the ground to be fitted up as a cage for prisoners of war and, in the second, several bombs for good measure were dropped on it. Once the war was over, herculean efforts were made to get the ground back into playing order for the 1946 season and improvements in the amenities have been made every year since then, notably in the winter of 1954-55, when the brave new terracing on the gasometer side of the ground was built. Today the Oval has become a spectator's joy and is no longer spectator's regret.

The great gasometer remains, lonely as Kanchenjunga and even more unconquerable. The correct name for this gargantuan cheese-shaped object is a gas-holder, but a gasometer by any other name would not instantly evoke nostalgic visions of the Oval. There is a cluster, or carbuncle, of gasometers, consisting of one tall one and two (or is it three?) stumpier ones and in the old days I was never quite sure whether it was the same one that always dwarfed the others or whether they took it in turns to stand on tip-toe to watch the cricket.

By 1955 the seating and spacing inside the ground had been immeasurably improved, and the great blocks of handsome new flats rising round the ground like a circular mountain range now fit in with Archbishop Tenison's Grammar School and add a clean, civilised air to the place that was hardly there in the old days. You miss the clang of the old trams in Harleyford Road, but in the realm of creature comforts everything in every way has grown better and better.

The first county match I saw at the Oval was in 1913, the summer before the one in which the first war started. Sitting on a hard wooden bench, I watched Yorkshire opening purposefully with Rhodes and that powerful batsman, B. B. Wilson. When these two had tired the bowlers, Hirst came in and hammered them as only Hirst could. There is no one now who pulls as fiercely as Hirst then did. Hendren, half a generation later, was the nearest, but he had not Hirst's shoulders. I did not see the rest of the game, though I learned from the newspapers of the next day or two that Yorkshire had won by an innings. The great thing was that I had seen Hirst swing gloriously into action—swing is the *mot juste*—and that was a lively consolation for a Yorkshire lad in London.

A twelve-month from that date, in what was to be the last Surrey v. Yorkshire match for five years, Surrey turned the tables and won by an inings. I did not see the game and no doubt to watch a Yorkshire drubbing would have given me pain, but, considering the matter after the lapse of years, it is obvious that I must have missed one of the batting feasts of the century: Hayward, 116; Hobbs, 202; Hayes, 134. Anyone who watched those three centuries must have been almost blinded. He might well have felt that he on honeydew had fed and drunk the milk of paradise. It was almost as though cricket, soon to sink below the horizon for five cruel years, was determined to leave its faithful followers in the gleam of a golden sunset.

II

The early Yorkshire matches at the Oval fade far back into the mists of time. There was the almost legendary appearance of Ephraim Lockwood, that truly 'anointed clodhopper' from Lascelles Hall, who turned out as a substitute, went in first with his Uncle John, and batted like a veteran. It was Lascelles Hall against the world. He made 91 and as he walked away from the wicket, tired but happy, the puzzled but good-natured Oval crowd cheered him with good humour and a little awe. Who was this boy? Where did he come from? He seemed such a slip of a lad that he looked, in classic phrase, 'fitter to eat a penny cake than play cricket.'

That was in 1868, but in 1877 there was a game in which Jupp (Old Juppy) and that glorious hitter, Walter Read, piled up 200, a partnership of a size almost unheard of in those days, and Tom Emmett, whose brow was wet with honest sweat in his efforts to dislodge them, was heard to murmur: 'Them two has took root!' And there was the queer 'gaslight' match of a dozen years later, when lights were lit in the pavilion and one by one the gas-lamps twinkled into life along the Harleyford Road. The run-stealers (and everybody else) flickered to and fro in the gloom and the winning hit was made in almost complete darkness as seven o'clock struck.

On the whole, Surrey seem to have had slightly the better of their yearly battles. In 1898, which was Rhodes's first season, Surrey won crushingly by an innings and 272. The following year saw a game that was not so much a game as a fantastic orgy of run-getting, in which 1,255 runs were

G

made and only seventeen men out. Yorkshire's score was 704 and Surrey's was 551 for seven and the morning and the evening were the third day. Wainwright made 228 and Hirst 186, while for Surrey Abel's score was 193 and Hayward's 273. These two had a useful little partnership of 448. Each side employed eight bowlers, and each wicket of the seventeen cost 73.82. But the most staggering fact of the match was not Hayward's 273, but the energy of Tom Richardson, whose figures unbelievably were:

overs, 58.1; maidens, 15; runs, 152; wickets, 5.

I have often doubted the importance of figures, but surely no flight of oratory, no stanza of lofty verse could pay so eloquent a tribute to Tom's indestructible endurance. Quite apart from anything else he may have done in the field, I calculate that he must have galloped at least four miles, running up to the wicket.

Ten years later Yorkshire were cut to pieces by ' Razor ' Smith and Rushby. Their score was the most abysmal in their history: 26, to which ' Lonzo ' Drake contributed a heroic nine. I should probably have run away, shuddering, if I had witnessed the debacle. I was about fourteen at the time, and the thing would have had all the horror of a public execution.

III

Between the wars the Oval saw a mixed bag of victories by (a) Surrey, (b) Yorkshire and (c) rain. Besides the weather, a further cause of drawn games was high scoring, in which the rival pairs of twins, Hobbs and Sandham and Holmes and Sutcliffe were the culprits, though scoring never again attained to the fantastic heights it had reached in 1899. It was in 1920 that I first saw Herbert Sutcliffe and the sight was a revelation. In the game I saw E. R. Wilson, by means of a mild scholarly kind of delivery, take five Surrey wickets for 29. He did not so much seem to be getting them out as rather fastidiously correcting their homework. But the man who instantly caught the eye and captured the imagination was a calm young fellow with glossy black hair who was the only batsman on either side in either innings to remain unperturbed by the venom of the wicket. That young man and I were born in the same year and, while my own hair has turned a particularly inartistic shade of off-white, his still remains smoothly and suavely black. This unruffled quality comes from an unruffled mind : from a heaven-sent ability not to worry about the state of the wicket. Surrey won an exciting game by 31 runs, but Sutcliffe won my unquenchable admiration. Two years later I watched him, from the same hard bench, compile a massive total of 232, but I doubt if this was as grand an innings as his 62 and 59 in the earlier game.

Since the second war there has been consistently level pegging; Surrey won deservedly in 1952 and 1953, but in 1954 Yorkshire inflicted on the home side one of their very few defeats in their four successive championships. This was made possible partly by a remarkable bowling performance by young Ray Illingworth and partly by a buccaneering innings by Lester who, in a manner rare among modern batsmen, started as he meant to go on, and went on until he had attacked, rammed and sunk the bowling with all hands. There has often seemed to be in Lester something of the gay attitude of David Denton; indeed, on his day, Lester has all the attributes of Lucky Denton except his luck.

IV

But, after all, the doughtiest deeds of Yorkshiremen at the Oval were not done in the name of their county alone. There were Yorkshiremen in the fatal Oval Test of 1882 which was the origin of the famous joke about the Ashes which, as *Wisden* somewhat acidly observed in 1896, ' *is now growing a little thin.*' George Ulyett batted soundly and was able afterwards to claim : ' We looked like getting 'em easy enough, while the Doctor and me were in.' George, who was not called Happy Jack for nothing, was perfectly good-tempered about it. W.G.'s comment was a trifle testy : ' Well, I got thirty-six; you'd have thought the rest of 'em could have managed as many between 'em.' And the ultimate culprit was Ted Peate, the founder and spiritual ancestor of Yorkshire's great line of slow-left-handers—Peel, Rhodes, Verity and Wardle—who was a highly intelligent bowler, but hardly the ideal No. 11. Coming in last with ten runs still needed he swiped at his first ball, hit a rocketing two, swiped at his second ball, missed it and was bowled. Thus England were all out and the first Ashes match lost by seven runs, while C. T. Studd, that highly competent all-rounder, was left not out without receiving a ball. Cross-examined as to the reasons for his rash, importunate act, Peate gave the classic reply: ' I couldn't trust Mr. Studd.'

Everybody knows of the historic last-wicket stand (' We'll get 'em in singles, Wilfred ') between Hirst and Rhodes in the most famous of all Test matches, Jessop's match in 1902; what seldom receives its due meed of praise is Hirst's heroic effort in the first innings when, gamely supported by Lockwood, he saved the follow-on, against all likelihood, and made the splendours of the second innings possible.

There was the part played by Sutcliffe and the same ageless Rhodes in England's memorable victory in 1926, the last rubber won on these shores until the recovery of the Ashes, under a Yorkshire captain, in 1953. And, equally memorable, there was that England captain's innings (he was fifteen years younger then) in 1938 which out-Bradmaned Bradman and has remained a record, isolated, gigantic and monumental as the great gasometer itself. Leonard Hutton has never made 364 again, which is probably a good thing, but he has come a long way since those days : further than any other professional cricketer has ever done. Of his profession he has been both a stable pillar and a handsome ornament, and such ill-will as resides in my composition I reserve almost exclusively for those who do not appreciate this man's true worth. It is the earnest supplication of all cricket-lovers, both in Yorkshire and in lands less blest, that the ironic gods who have bestowed on him so many gifts and well-deserved honours with one hand should call a truce to the lumbar afflictions they have wished on him with the other.*

---

* Since these lines were written, the fell ailment has done its worst and Hutton has retired from the field. Later Her Majesty the Queen has done her gracious best and a high honour has been conferred where it was well deserved.

CHAPTER 8

THE BOBBY-DAZZLERS

I

EVEN IN an egalitarian universe there is one glory of the sun and another of the moon. In every age in every field of endeavour there are the artists, the warriors, the skilled craftsmen, the hewers of wood and drawers of water. You can fit most of the cricketers you know into one or other of these categories. But, again in every age, there are one or two whom you can no more confine to a category than you can pin a live butterfly to a card. There are those who, out and beyond the laws of sound workmanship or even of stylistic elegance, dazzle the eye, enchant the mind, and remain for ever as magic in the memory. Such, half a century ago, was Victor Trumper, who had three strokes for every ball, and who thought no bowler could bowl, anyway; such was K. S. Ranjitsinhji, the renowned Ranji, whose bat was the wand of an oriental wizard; such was K. L. Hutchings, who on a sunny morning could predict: 'I shall get a century today!' And such in our own day has been Denis Compton (on Denis Compton's day) whose attitude towards the spectator and even, at an advanced stage of a vintage Compton innings, towards the ball itself, can be likened to that of the famed singer of songs of Araby: 'to cheat thee of a sigh and charm thee to a tear . . .'

There are others, but not many. Those who have charmed me are the charmers indeed. They came as Mark Antony protested he did not, to steal away your hearts. Sir James Barrie once said of his favourite cricketer: 'He doesn't hit the ball: he just whispers to it where to go and it goes.' We have all seen Compton do just that. These rare cricketers are the music-makers, the dreamers of dreams. These are the players who can bring to the crowd of otherwise anxious and oppressed citizens a touch of freedom and a ripple of delight.

They can distil pure sunshine from a brief summer day. When they are at the wicket the sun itself seems to take on more warmth and brightness.

II

The first time I saw David Denton was when Uncle Walter took me to Bradford to see Yorkshire play Gloucestershire long, long ago, half a hundred years at least. It was a day of temperamental weather and two or three times the players had to scamper for the pavilion. But as soon as the sun came out, Denton came out with it and, amiably resuming his task as though it had never been interrupted, smote the bowling, hip and thigh. His partner, my fellow-townsman Jimmy Rothery, batted well, but Denton played as though it was his business to show how ridiculously easy the bowling was. (In point of fact, the bowling was excellent.) I can see him now, stepping briskly down the pavilion steps, neat, dapper, not a big man, light on his pins as a ballet-dancer. Time after time he late-cut Jessop, who was bowling very fast, so that the ball skimmed like a swallow past third man; and Dennett, who at the other end was bowling slowly and with infinite cunning, he cut and hooked with a sort of frivolous fury that made fielding anywhere on the leg side an occupation that should have carried danger money with it. As for the other bowlers, he treated them with amiable scorn and hit them just anywhere.

' By . . .' murmured Uncle Walter, ' he's a bobby-dazzler.'

When Denton had made a hundred, a ball grazed his wicket without taking the bails off and, as though to salute his good fortune, he went on to hit up another 72 with even more flippant effrontery.

' That's why they call him Lucky Denton,' said the man in the muffler sitting next to us.

' Never in this world,' retorted Uncle Walter. ' A man who goes for 'em like that deserves all the luck he can get.'

I thought so, too, and I think so still. Whether fortune favours the brave or not, the brave richly deserve that it should. The legend of Lucky Denton pursued him all his life and it was commonly reported that as he strode to the wicket with his quick, gay, let-me-get-at-'em step, fielding captains said ruefully to their team-mates: 'Come on, lads, who's going to miss him first?'

But if he had luck, it was the luck of the bold adventurer. He approached the crease, not apologetically, not meekly, but in a spirit of happy hostility. I once heard an old Yorkshire cricketer say: 'Anybody can have a bit of fun at Scarborough, but Denton was playing at Scarborough all the time.' The fact that this was said with a faint air of disapproval does not invalidate its essential truth. Denton brought the spirit of festival even to the death-grapple of a Roses match, and he would hook a Brearley bumper 'off his eyebrows' in a manner that set Old Trafford in a roar. There were few in Denton's day who began every innings in that spirit and there are fewer still in this far-from-brave new world. If Denton attacked the bowling from the first ball, he was bound to put a few hearts into a few mouths; he was even bound to get a duck or two, but it is outside credibility and common sense that a batsman who made over 36,000 in twenty-odd years, including 69 centuries, should have attained these happy objectives through a long series of snicks, mishits and dropped catches.

If he was occasionally lucky at the wicket, he needed no luck in the field. In an age rich in fine fieldsmen, Denton was outstanding in 'the country' or at deep third man. Nowadays a slow bowler gets most of his wickets (if he gets them) with the odd leg-before-wicket decision, but batsmen then were more audacious and *c Denton b Rhodes* was a fate that bolder spirits often brought upon themselves. For them it was a short life, if a gay one, for David had wonderfully safe hands. If Denton at some early point in his innings was dropped, his team-mates used to smile; it was all part of the game. But if Denton, that impeccable fieldsman, himself dropped a catch, the mishap was so rare that the whole side stood aghast. It was like the temporary fall of an angel from grace. There is a legend that once in a game at Lord's Denton dropped, not merely one catch, but two. The whole fielding side went to pieces and an old Yorkshire player who was watching—could it have been Tom Emmett—burst into tears. Or so they say.

In the deep he was a lovely sight to see: the sure anticipation, the speedy making of the ground, the clean pick-up

and the long throw-in, apparently merged in a single movement; all these things were stamped with swiftness, accuracy
and grace. I can see him now: the longish, dryly humorous
face behind the heavy moustache of the period, the lithe form,
the air of eager desire for cheerfully violent action. It is a
picture you do not readily forget.

He was born in 1874, so when I first saw him he must have
been thirty-one and in his prime. That was, or so everyone
thought at the time, his greatest season, when he made 2,405
runs, and on the strength of it appeared in *Wisden* as one
of the five Cricketers of the Year. But seven years later, when
he was thirty-eight, he had another season of happy run-
gathering, hitting a couple of double centuries and reduc-
ing bowlers all over the country to a state bordering on
impotence.

He was twenty years old when he first played for Yorkshire
in 1894, a great year for the county, in which Herbert Sutcliffe and J. B. Priestley were born. (On the other hand, I was
born myself in that year, so it works both ways.) He had
played quite good cricket before he reached the county side.
Born at Thorner, near Wakefield, his talents brandished themselves so conspicuously that he played for a works team at
the age of fourteen. By the time he was seventeen he was tried
for the Yorkshire colts, and at eighteen he was top of his
club's batting and bowling averages.

There were no startling developments in his first year for
the county, but in 1895 he flashed out with the first of many
fine scores against Lancashire and from that moment his
White Rose cap was a certainty. After that he went happily
forward, compiling his thousand runs a year with inevitable,
but never monotonous, regularity. Twenty-one times he made
his annual thousand; three of these he turned into 2,000.
Steadily he advanced from the middle of the batting order
to No. 4 and then permanently to the key post of No. 3.
What a menacing muster that Yorkshire batting order must
have appeared to opposition bowlers: Brown, Tunnicliffe,
Denton, with the threat of Jackson and Hirst to come
after.

Denton toured South Africa twice, in 1905-06 and 1909-10,
and in the latter jaunt he was one of the mainstays of the
batting. At one period he scored three successive centuries,

the third one in a Test, on those fast South African wickets. The faster the wicket, the better he liked it. He revelled in all the lightnings that Kotze and the other South African fast bowlers could hurl at him and the 'tricks and manners' of their sinister googly-spinning comrades left him unshaken.

Altogether he played in eleven Tests, ten against South Africa, and only one against Australia. Here his reputation as fortune's darling acted paradoxically in his disfavour. 'No', I can imagine the chairman of selectors saying, 'not Denton. Lucky he may be, but how can we be sure that the Australian fielders know about it? You can't trust those fellows to drop him . . .'

Lucky Denton was unlucky in being contemporary with Johnny Tyldesley. Now Tyldesley was a modest and friendly soul and the last person in the world to go around singing: 'Anything you can do, I can do better.' The fact remains, however, that Tyldesley possessed and practised Denton's arts and skills to a degree that was a shade superior. There was no Yorkshireman who did not admire Johnny Tyldesley. They could give the enemy, even the Lancastrian enemy, his due. So it fell out that Johnny won and held England's No. 3 position. Yorkshiremen thought that room might have been found for both of them, but then again the chairman of selectors might have replied: 'Very well, we like Denton as much as you do, but as a matter of interest, whom are you going to leave out: Fry, MacLaren, Hayward, Spooner, or this rather promising young chap, Hobbs?'

The plain facts are that (a) there was a prodigal wealth of great batsmen in Denton's time and (b) a player with Denton's rich range of strokes and gay attacking temperament could walk into any England Test team of today.

It was in his only Test against Australia that Lucky Denton suffered his unluckiest blow. He was not the first, as he will not be the last, Englishman to suffer ill fortune at Leeds, where, before the crowd that loved him, in the year of 1905 when he could virtually do nothing wrong, he was out for a duck in the first innings to a stroke for which he probably kicked himself all round the dressing-room. In the second innings, he had just set off his first happy fireworks when he was accounted for by one of those miracle matches that *nobody* can account for. Lucky Denton was as unlucky in being out to that catch as if he had been knocked down by a motor car on the pavement outside the ground.

After the first war, at the age of forty-five, he was batting almost as well as ever, and his 209 not out against Worcestershire in 1920 was as brilliant as anything he had ever done. But bad health attacked him. Soon after his retirement, he suffered a more serious illness. For a time he was Yorkshire's scorer and then, after an operation had restored him to vigour, he became a First Class umpire, an honoured member of the most honourable of professions.

He would not perhaps have been a candidate for the timeless cosmic eleven, like Hobbs or Rhodes or Bradman or Trumper, but, studying Yorkshire's proud and rugged history, he must have been among the half-dozen most popular players in that mighty muster roll. As an entertainer pure and simple, of the type now, alas, almost defunct, he was unsurpassed. I can think of hardly any cricketer who, to schoolboys from eight to eighty, has, in a lifetime, given more pure, unadulterated pleasure than did David Denton. There is not enough of this pleasure today and there are not nearly enough of the men who can give it.

III

Once the demands of pure patriotism have been satisfied, a man has a right to be tolerant and even, in a burst of liberal-mindedness, to admit that there are other cricket counties besides his own. Some counties inspire a kindly feeling because they are often easily beaten; some invite fierce battle and are profoundly respected; and some are composed of such pleasant fellows that, win, lose or draw, the game carries its own enjoyment.

Sometimes there have been counties which, through all the changing scenes of cricket's life, glittered with great names like an illuminated scroll. There was, for example, Gloucestershire, home of the three Graces, Jessop, Hammond, Charlie Barnett, and Tom Graveney; not so much a county as a constellation.

And there was Kent. I have of course, no drop of southern blood, but, as a boy, I never ' minded ' Kent. As you were, I minded Kent once. That was the year in which Kent slipped to the top of the table, because Gloucestershire beat Yorkshire by one run. 'Gloucestershire,' said Old Ebor at the time, 'received hosts of congratulatory telegrams, many of which, oddly enough, emanated from Kent.' It was that *oddly enough* which stuck in my throat.

But, away from the noise of battle, Kent was a county any boy might like. Where Yorkshire had strength, Kent had charm. I have no illusions as to which is more important, but what is life without a little sweetness and light? There was in 'my' time something about the very names of the players that suggested the cherry orchards and the hopfields of that corner of our country which is called the Garden of England : J. R. Mason and R. N. R. Blaker, C. J. Burnup and the peerless K. L. Hutchings.

But the greatest of Kentish names was and, I think, always will be Frank Woolley. What does the name call to your mind? A tall slim graceful figure at the wicket : he lifts his bat high, with what at first seems a nonchalant swing, so easy that it looks almost indolent until you have heard the bullet-like smack with which the ball hits the pickets; and almost careless until, hour after hour, you have watched the precision of the strokes that take the middle of the bat. It is a picture of mingled power and charm.

We all have our favourite left-handers. On the whole, they are a lovable but lumpy lot. My own favourite—for me Woolley is outside comparison—was Maurice Leyland, a tower of strength to England, a Rock of Gibraltar on two sturdy Yorkshire legs. Whenever England appeared to be in danger of lying at the foot of a proud conqueror, Leyland was a major part of the resistance movement. There never was a more reliable resister. Anybody who underrated his value must have been a perfect fool. And, leaping out of our context for a moment, the same goes for those who underrate Trevor Bailey. But was Leyland beautiful? In his character, yes; in his broad, cheerful, all-right-then-bowl-me-out-if-you-can kind of smile, certainly. But as an æsthetic symbol of the sublime and the beautiful, hardly.

Who was the most prolific of lefthanders? Figures never lie—well, hardly ever—and they will tell you that, again after Woolley, it was Mead. A near-invincible batsman and a sterling character was Philip Mead, sheet anchor of Hamp-

shire as Leyland was of Yorkshire. In his career he scored
over 55,000 runs, a total which exceeded Grace's, Hammond's
and Sutcliffe's and was only beaten by Hobbs, Woolley himself, and Hendren. Year after year Mead went on, a standing
menace to every county's attack. He was so difficult to dislodge and his career was so long that he must have broken
more bowlers' hearts than ever Bradman did. It was said
that, when Bradman had knocked up 300 or so, he would
consider giving the bowlers a chance, but not Philip. I speak
with prejudice. He was the only batsman who ever came near
to defying Yorkshire bowling almost permanently. His man-
nerisms—the pulling down of the cap, the steps back towards
square leg, and all the rest of them—were known, and occasionally parodied, wherever cricket is played. The eccentricities
of the eminent are always puzzling. Why did Mead pull
down his cap and take the little steps backwards? And why,
when you come to think of it, did Omar Khayyám want a
loaf of bread beneath the bough? The book of verse, yes;
the wine, certainly; the 'thou,' indubitably; but what did
he want with all that intolerant deal of bread? But we
digress. All honour to Philip Mead, a man and a cricketer of
immense worth. But as a model for Phidias the sculptor, he
lacked something.

I think I have seen most of the great Australian left-
handers of my lifetime: Joe Darling and Clem Hill, punish-
ing leg-hitters both, especially of fast bowling; Warren Bardsley and Vernon Ransford, obstinate defenders and moun-
tainous scorers; and Arthur Morris and Neil Harvey, engag-
ing performers who since the second war have given us rare
pleasure (and trouble). But none of these had, or has, the grace,
the felicity, the consummate artistry of a Frank Woolley.

He first played for Kent in 1906, when he was nineteen.
In his first county match, which was at Old Trafford, he
missed three catches (all beastly ones), got a duck, and took
one wicket for over a hundred runs. But in the second innings
he made 64 and won himself another trial. In his next game
he captured six wickets for 39, and in his third, at the Oval,
he bowled the great Tom Hayward, hit 72, took five more
wickets, and then by coolness and courage at the vital moment,
carried his side to a thrilling one-wicket victory. The Oval
crowd, who invariably react to drama, swarmed on to the

ground and carried him off. By the time his admirers had done their work, he was so battered and bewildered that he tumbled into his bath with one boot on. That was the beginning of a happy career which, broken only by the first world war, lasted until 1938.

Figures do not explain everything but, over a period of thirty years, a generation in a man's or a country's history, they are scarcely negligible. In that time Woolley made nearly 59,000 runs, being only surpassed by Hobbs, and took over 2,000 wickets. He scored a thousand runs a season twenty-eight times, a fantastic sequence, equalled only by the mono-lithic figure (and gigantic figures) of W.G. himself. In all Woolley scored 145 centuries and did the 'double' eight times. The astonishing element in his doubles was that four of them involved 2,000 runs and three of them were achieved in successive seasons. His 305 against Tasmania in 1911-12 is the highest score made by a member of a touring side in Australia. His bowling figures of ten for 49 against the Aus-tralians at the Oval in 1912 constitute a Test match record. I saw that game and have described it elsewhere. It was the wettest of weeping summers. Woolley bowled at the Austra-lians practically all the time, with the great Sidney Barnes at the other end in the first innings and Harry Dean of Lancashire in the second.

His total of 64 Test match appearances, 52 of which were consecutive, has only been surpassed by Hammond (85) and Hutton (72). He was in the Players' side against the Gentle-men fourteen years in succession. On the basis of any figures you care to examine, he was a nonesuch. Even his modest bag of nearly a thousand catches is bigger than that of any fields-man who was not a wicket-keeper.

The two most dazzling displays I ever saw him give were in the Lord's Test of 1921 when he defied Warwick Arm-strong's remorseless conquerors. As for the twenty to thirty thousand other persons present on each of the three days, those two innings, I will swear, were the best they had ever seen, too. Against the thunder of Gregory and the lightning of Macdonald, not to mention the Machiavellian cunning of Mailey, Woolley stood almost alone. In the first innings he received very little help from anybody and, in the second, there was only Tennyson, who stayed nobly with him for a time, and it was sad that he could not, like his grandfather's brook, go on for ever. In the two melancholy processions Woolley was like a gay wedding guest at a couple of funerals. His scores were 95 and 93 and none of his 145 centuries can have risen to such grandeur. While England was on its beam ends, he was on his toes. It was hard to know which to admire most : his gallantry or his gaiety. Generously he gave of both.

He was a delight to watch because he played the game of cricket in the best way cricket can be played. He gave to the game his grace, his artistry, his effortless power. Because he has honoured the game, the game honours him.

IV

Cardus called him ' Mercutio ' because he would not fight by the book of arithmetic and he was known to his contemporary Australians as ' the Governor-General.' It was K. L. Hutchings who so christened him and his wife once heard two schoolboys discussing the reason. ' Why do they call Macartney the Governor-General ?' ' Because he's so cocky, of course !' Let us by all means describe his highest quality as a superb combination of courage and confidence, but he would not have minded in the least your calling it cockiness. It was in fact sheer cheek, uninhibited, unadulterated, magnificent cheek. As an honorary governor-general, he was short, sharp and authoritative and without question was the only Australian between Trumper and Bradman, the mere whisper of whose name could draw a crowd.

There was cricket in Macartney's blood, for his grandfather had been a famous bowler in games against early English touring teams. In his early schooldays the young Macartney committed certain acts of truancy in support of the theory that the bat was mightier than the cane. He even came a little later under a headmaster so insensate to the call of higher things that he stopped school cricket for the summer term because of the foolish notion that the boys had done no work for their examinations. In righteous scorn Macartney abandoned the academic world for commerce and took his first job with a produce merchant in Sydney's dockland at seven-and-six a week.

Like many an eager lad before and since, he battled his way up the various rungs of Sydney's grade cricket ladder paying his first club subscription in two half-guinea instalments. Grade cricket is a severe testing-ground and, of the many fine players called, only the few that are better than the best are chosen to rise to inter-State and Test level. Macartney had two strings to his bow: besides being a furiously aggressive right-hand bat, he was a baffling left-hand slow bowler and his supreme confidence told him that if he did not come off in one way he would come off in another.

He played for Australia from the 1907-08 season against A. O. Jones's side without much of a break until 1926. This included tours to England in 1909, 1912, 1921 and 1926. He did little in his first tour, did much better, especially with the ball, in his second. His Test figures for both batting and bowling over this long period are impressive.

No. of Tests	Inns.	N.O.	Runs	Hghst Sc.	100s.	50s.	Av.
35	55	4	2,132	170	7	9	41.80

Wickets	Runs	5 wkts. inn.	Average	Catches
45	1,240	1	27.55	17

But, handsome as they are, the statistics give only a sketch of the full story. They do not show the superb combination of eye, hand and foot which made him an almost miraculous punisher of fast bowling and they do not tell of the century that he scored before lunch at Leeds in 1926. Even Macartney himself, laconic in speech as he was dazzling in action, described this game as rather sensational. He went in after Bardsley had been caught off the first ball of the match and was himself missed off the third. After this escape he played an innings which, apart from one or two classic innings by Trumper, Jessop and Bradman and one glorious exhibition by K. L. Hutchings, must have been the most brilliant display of aggressive cricket ever seen in a Test match. 'Other writers and witnesses,' Macartney reported afterwards, ' have been pleased to say that my innings that day was the best they ever saw, but I am only going to remark that I made up my mind to attack and keep on attacking.'

Nor can any figures fully show the staggering quality in the victory of the 1921 Australians over Notts on the second

day of the match by an innings and 500 runs. (If I believed
in the use of exclamation marks I should consider the fore-
going sentence worthy of two.)

W. Bardsley, b Richmond	....	0
T. J. E. Andrews, c Coates, b Barratt	...	29
C. G. Macartney, lbw b Hardstaff	......	345
J. M. Taylor, c Whysall, b Barratt	......	50
C. E. Pellew, c Oates, b Barratt	....	100
J. M. Gregory, not out	....	8
Extras	....	9

Total for 5 wickets 541

Eight of the Notts players had a turn with the ball and,
because Pellew had hit 28 runs off Carr's one over, Macartney
got the idea that his own rate of scoring must be lagging
behind his partner's. When, however, Pellew was caught at
the wicket after hitting 100 in 107 minutes, it was discovered
that Macartney had added 184 and that their happy partnership had progressed at the rate of nearly three runs a
minute. This was not only the champagne of cricket, it was
champagne of the noblest vintage.

Macartney's high scores were by no means all made against
weaker bowling sides. Often he went in, when disaster had
occurred, to retrieve his side's fortune, but never did he accept
a defensive role. It was, I think, Marshal Foch who was
asked what he would do if his centre caved in and both his
flanks were turned. (I cannot think who, or with what
object, would ask a great general such a damn-fool question.)
' *Alors*,' said Marshal Foch, ' *j'attaquerai*.' That was Macartney's constant attitude and his motto was : Defiance, not
defence. However much the bowlers might be in the ascen-
dant when Macartney came in, when he had finished with
them they were the under-dogs. Describing the most famous
of his centuries he said : ' I felt like it and consequently I
went for everything.' But he almost always felt like it and
he almost always went for everything. Small wonder that
he favoured three-day Tests. Given a couple of Macartneys
on each side, you could probably have had two-day Tests.
What he lacked in height he made up in swift, instinctive

footwork and his square cutting and cover driving surprised the fieldsmen in much the same way as the old photographer's magnesium pistol startled its victims. As you blinked the ball hit the boundary boards. Macartney must have been the only batsman in the world who could regularly pass Jack Hobbs's right or left hand in the covers.

At the end of Macartney's last Sheffield Shield match in 1927 he received an ovation equal even to that which greeted his hurricane 151 at Leeds. So great was the desire of his fellow-cricketers to honour him that the stately Woodfull, who had never hit a six in his first-class career before, went berserk and hit two. The crowd loved Macartney and Macartney, though he played to please himself and not them, loved the crowd.

His humour was like a dry Australian wine. He once described a tour of Rome as 'the hardest day's sight-seeing I ever suffered.' He said of Oldfield's wicket-keeping that you never knew he was there till he had you out. Once when, a year or two ago, someone at Sydney Oval tried to draw him into an argument, 'I wouldn't know,' he replied, 'I only came here to see Toshack bat.'

When he retired he did a certain amount of writing about cricket matches for the press and was quietly conscientious in doing the job. He said there were things you could see from the press-box that you could not see from the field of play, and vice versa. Modestly he confessed that he found his new job interesting, but though he was reporting Test matches every day, he felt no urge to rush down and join in.

'Except once,' he added. 'The game *called* for hitting and the bowling *wanted* hitting, but the batsmen wouldn't hit. For two pins I'd have gone down into the middle an belted 'em!' Too right, he would.

He was, is and always will be a most unostentatious person, but his attitude to life is similar to that of one of the noblest figures in this island's history:

> He either fears his fate too much
>   Or his deserts are small
> Who fears to put it to the touch
>   To win or lose it all.

H

V

When Adam delved and Eve span, who was then the gentleman? And when Bradman retired, who was then the greatest Australian batsman? Was it that technicolorful individualist, Sidney Barnes, who at any given moment might be jumping over the gate or kicking over the traces? Or was it that handsome batsman and charming person, Arthur Morris? Certainly Morris was a bobby-dazzler in 1948, though he was hardly the same world-beater in 1953 and 1955. English players will suggest that the answer to the question is a slim, raven-haired young man named Neil Harvey. He first played for Australia when he was nineteen and when he toured England with Bradman in 1948, he was the baby of the side. Born in an industrial suburb of Melbourne, he came of a cricket-addicted family; three of his brothers have played for their State, and one of them was chosen for his country against Walter Hammond's 1946-47 team.

Baby of the team Neil might be, but he shouldered responsibility like a seasoned warrior. It was not so much that he scored a century in his first Test against England (he had already made 153 in his second Test against India); his splendour shone in this: that, like Trumper and Macartney, he would accept no apprenticeship to servitude, but started with beautiful strokes from the first ball he received. When the wicket and the attack were easy he would let loose a star-shower of exuberant gaiety, a golden rain of fours and sixes. But when the pitch was wicked and the attack fierce, he played as though he had years of ripe experience behind him. In the first match against Yorkshire, one of the only two games that Australia ever looked like losing, he stepped into the breach when his side, wanting 60 to win, had lost six wickets for 31 to Smailes and Wardle. Harvey did not defend; he hit Australia's way out of trouble, and finished the game with a colossal six.

He did nothing startling at home in 1948-49 but in 1949-50 on his first South African tour it was roses, roses all the way. In Tests he made 660 runs with an average of 132, including four centuries, the most gorgeous of which was 151 not out, scored after Australia had been routed for 75 by Tayfield in the first innings and had been set a seemingly impossible number of runs to win. In the whole tour he made eight hundreds and his aggregate was over 1,500, a tremendous total for a short tour.

In no season has he quite recaptured the artistic fluency and rich variety of his South African tour, but he has been at all times Australia's most potentially dangerous batsman. In 1950-51 he had a Test average of 40 against Freddy Brown's touring side and of 55 in Sheffield Shield matches. In the following year he had a rather poor Test season against the West Indian tourists and an even poorer one in State games, but in 1952-53 he came back to power with a vengeance, for although Jack Cheetham's South Africans had a startlingly successful trip, they did not achieve their success at the personal expense of Neil Harvey, who in Tests scored 834, a total that approached even Bradman's record. There was simply no limit to the praise showered upon, and merited by, his power and elegance.

In England in 1953 he was not satisfied with his performance, though you might have imagined he was very hard to please, for he made ten centuries, most of them of coruscating brilliance, including an innings of 180 at Swansea of which Welshmen still speak in hushed voices. His aggregate was over 2,000 and his average just under 66, but in Tests he made only 365. This was but 19 less than Hassett's, the highest Test total of the tour, but it was not enough for Neil; his desire was to dominate.

It was much the same when he played against Hutton's men of 1954-55. His Test aggregate of 354 was not merely Australia's highest; it was over a hundred more than the next man's. But it did not put him on the winning side. In the first Test, which marked Australia's solitary victory, he made 162, and in the second he fought, almost alone, a splendid rear-guard action, playing what must have been one of the supreme innings of his life. While wickets fell monotonously, he hit with enormous power, farming the bowling and keeping hope alive. When his last partner fell to a semi-miraculous catch by Evans, England had won a desperate game by 38 runs and Harvey had carried out his bat for 92.

England won the Ashes in 1953 and retained them in safe custody in 1954-55. It is Australia's clear intent to win them

back. Neil Harvey's comparative, repeat comparative, failure
in the last Tests means that a rod is being laid up in pickle
for England. Neil Harvey, the most talented and attractive
left-hander now playing, has got it in for us. He will yet
spread delight among spectators all over this country. But
England will suffer.

VI

Of all the bobby-dazzlers that have glittered in the Caribbean sunshine the most dazzling of all was Leary Constantine.
Indeed, in the matter of sheer dazzle for dazzle's sake, Constantine was probably the bobbiest dazzler of them all. Without plumbing the profounder etological depths of the effect
of climate on character we might reasonably say that the
green and gold of the West Indies hardly form the most
appropriate background for dullness, stonewalling and that
form of peaceful co-existence in which the bowling lion and
the batting lamb sometimes lie down together in more tem-
perate climes. In the West Indies the batsman hits the ball
into the treetops, even at the risk of dislodging the rest of his
family therefrom; the fast bowler bowls with all his eager
heart and soul, and the slow bowler calls to his aid the wiles
of the traditional wagon-load of monkeys. Gusto and gaiety
are in the blood.

If we ask who was the greatest of all West Indian batsmen,
the answer might well be George Headley, a prince of the
unorthodox and as quick as Macartney in his footwork. And
what of the feared and formidable W-trio? I should say that
Weekes was the most consistent run-getter, Walcott, if only
from his immense physical strength, the hardest hitter, and
Worrell the most alluring to the aesthetic eye.

Frank Worrell comes from the sunny sugar-laden island of
Barbados and in his style seems to convey both the beauty
and the languor of his native isle, where, just to add a touch
to the gaiety, the natives speak with a rich Irish brogue.
As he strolls absent-mindedly to the wicket you half expect a
hidden orchestra to play a signature tune, *Sleepy Lagoon*. He
first played for his island as a schoolboy of seventeen and his
talent was for slow bowling. He did not come into prominence
as a batsman until a couple of years later. Those of us who

sit at home at ease at Lord's or the Oval tend to think of a touring side as a single entity. Australians are Australians and, behind their closed ranks, we see little of the fierce faction fights of New South Wales v. Victoria; West Indians are West Indians and we do not ponder on the island battles of Barbados v. Trinidad, which spark off under the blue skies the electric atmosphere generated in a Roses match under grey. What started the intense rivalry between these sister islands is a mystery and an even deeper mystery is the reason why the natives of Barbados speak with a rich Irish accent. Do not ask me.

In a Barbados v. Trinidad match in 1944 Worrell joined John Goddard, later to be captain of the victorious touring side of 1950, at the fall of the fourth wicket. Together they went on and on, as though time had stood still, until a score of 502 for the fifth wicket had made its gargantuan way to the record books. Not long afterwards the record was twice broken, but I cannot think that Worrell cared. The whole population of Barbados became delirious with delight and play finished ten minutes before time because the island people invaded the pitch to bestow plaudits and presents on their new hero.

From then on, apprehensive bowlers were to hear more and more of Frank Worrell. He came to England to play for Radcliffe in the Central Lancashire League and there broke all kinds of records. When his club released him to join the West Indies side touring England in 1950 he revelled in the fun. Here was the most brilliantly illuminated page so far in West Indian cricket history. The three W's made twenty centuries between them, many of them double ones for good measure, and although the summer of 1950, like every summer from 1949 to 1954 inclusive, was cold and wet and unfriendly, their presence brought a rainbow gleam across the dark sky. I was not lucky enough to see Worrell's magnificent 267 in the Nottingham Test, but I did see a small gem of an innings at Lord's when Worrell meandered lackadaisically to his fifty in the time most Test batsmen of today take to reach double figures. He began with three fours, each one of them a gem of purest ray serene, and seemed gently to contradict the old adage: more haste less speed. He achieved immense speed with no apparent haste whatsoever.

Worrell has not since produced—perhaps no one could produce—the radiant form of the 1950 tour. In Australia in 1951-52 he had a slightly unhappy time against Lindwall and Miller and when Hutton's team drew level in the thrilling rubber of 1953-54, Worrell was not one of the compilers of mammoth scores against them. Unfit in the first Test, he made a duck and 76 not out in the second, and nothing to speak of in the third and fifth. Only in the drawn fourth game did he give a true taste of his quality with 167 and 56. But sometimes a small score by Worrell can be as distinguished as a big one by almost anyone else. Size is not the final criterion of value, or pancakes would be worth more than pearls and Wordsworth's *Excursion* more than his sonnet on Milton.

There is an endearingly indolent quality about Worrell's every action and his friends say that they have to wake him every time it is his turn to bat. The stories of his dozing tendencies are no doubt exaggerated; otherwise Frank Worrell must be the most gifted somnambulist now in motion. But if any aspect of batsmanship can give pure pleasure, it is the lazy grace with which, at the last fraction of a second, he square-cuts a ball to the rails. His late cut has all the glory and last-moment suddenness of a tropical sunset. Long may his lazy sun shine . . .

VII

One of the worst beltings that English bowlers have ever bent to since Bradman's time was suffered from the bat of Roy McLean who, at Lord's in the second Test of the Springboks' 1955 tour, took them by the scruff of the neck and hit 142, including a six, off Statham at that, and fourteen fours. It was not an innings lit by sheer elegance in the Woolley manner; nor did it have a touch of Worrell's indolent grace. Rather was it in Macartney's vein. ('I felt like it and I went for everything.') McLean must have felt like it for he indeed went for everything. The Lord's crowd paid him tribute, none the less open-handed because it was a little rueful.

He was born twenty-six years ago in Pietermaritzburg, Natal's second largest town. At school he was one of those enviably gifted games-players who do everything well and appear to do everything easily. (He played cricket and rugger

for Natal before he was twenty and might well have played
in representative hockey, too.) When he visited England with
Dudley Nourse's 1951 Springboks, he and McGlew were the
babies of the side and probably its most dashing fieldsmen.
He did not quite reach his thousand runs on the tour but his
average of over 30 was highly creditable and his best scores,
including a hard-hit 88 against Yorkshire, were taken from
the strongest bowling. He played in only three Tests with an
average of 27.6.

In the giant-killing 1952-53 tour of Australia, McLean
was one of the leading Jacks. His aggregate was not massive.
He seemed to save his supreme efforts for vital moments of the
Tests, for while his average for the whole tour did not reach
25, in the Tests it was 41. Nor does this difference in figures
tell the whole truth, for the two innings that really mattered
were seen in the never-to-be-forgotten fifth Test at Melbourne,
when South Africa's astonishing victory made the rubber a
tie. Until half way through the game, the odds were all on
Australia, who won the toss and piled up a huge score,
including a fierce and nearly flawless 205 by Neil Harvey.
The Springboks made a defiant reply and the core of it was
a furiously hit 81 by McLean, including many fours and a
black eye. The black eye was a gift but the fours, which he
found more blessed to give than to receive, were hammered
past the fieldsmen in less than an hour and a half. Australia's
second attempt was not so carefree as the first had been but
even so South Africa were left just under 300 runs to win,
no piece of cake in the fourth innings.

The hardships inherent in this task were hardly lightened
by the early fall of the first wicket, but the Springboks fought
first stubbornly and then dashingly. On the last morning the
pitch was visibly cracking and it seemed to the South Africans
that they must make the runs quickly or for ever hold their
peace. Endean and Watkins hit hard and often and, when
McLean dashed out at the fall of the fourth wicket, he began
instantly to hit harder than either of them. Half a dozen
bowlers took their turn and took their punishment; Bill John-
ston received a harsher caning than ever he had had at
school. Peering at the bowling through his bruised eye, Mc-
Lean smote it as bowling has scarcely been smitten since
Jessop's time and, modestly assisted by the left-hander, Keith,

swept breathlessly to victory in a blaze of boundaries. His 76 was hit out of 106 in eighty minutes and contained fourteen fours. In the end it was not so much a blaze as a large-scale conflagration.

True, McLean, like all dazzlers, has his critics. They say that he is reckless and that he will slash wildly, too early on, at balls which he would have been better advised to treat with respect. Certainly in the final innings of the 1955 Oval Test he was out to a stroke which, if not a scandal, was at least a major indiscretion. And he had not done particularly well in the first innings, either. It is not much use arguing about this. The defenders are valuable; sometimes, like Trevor Bailey, they are invaluable. But the dazzlers are precious, because they are rare and grow rarer. Of course they are reckless, their tenure of the crease is tenuous. They are like Burns's snowfall in the river. ' A moment white—then melts for ever . . .' But my sympathies are with the dazzlers : they are the foes of dullness, the defiers of deadlock. Boldly they follow the old Spanish proverb : take your pleasure and pay for it.

In the home season of 1953-54 McLean scored South Africa's solitary Test century against the visiting New Zealanders. In the last match of the South African season before the Springboks left for England, he hit up 187 against Orange Free State in two and a half hours in an innings prodigal of fours and sixes. On his 1955 tour he was not the ' best ' batsman : the best, i.e. the most reliable, was the admirable McGlew, whose average of 58 was 20 more than McLean's. But of McLean's attractiveness there was no doubt. The great crowd that saw his 148 at Lord's will never forget it. They saw a great light. But, looking back, it is reasonable to assert that his unchallanged masterpiece was the hurricane which swept across Australian bowlers at Melbourne on the twelfth of February, 1953, and seized victory for a South African side which critics had said would not win a single game. The great crowd of Australians who saw this were unanimous. This was his finest hour.

When, in the last innings of the Oval Test in 1955, the Springboks were set a mere 244 to win, I could not think of any reason why they should not get them. While McGlew and Goddard were attempting a steady start, I am told that

I sat, glumly uncommunicative, breaking silence only to emit a hollow groan when Goddard was missed in the slips off Bailey. When the first two wickets fell at 28 and the third at 29, I came to life slowly and still silently, and when McLean was out l.b.w. to Laker, I am alleged by my daughter to have sat up and ejaculated : '*Now we shall win!*'

And this, whichever way you look at it, was a sincere tribute to a batsman, not in his finest hour, but at his worst moment.

CHAPTER 9

SMITH AND CO.

I

WHICH IS the largest family in cricket? I use the word
in the general, rather than the particular sense which
once caused Worcestershire to be known as Fostershire (H.K.,
R.E., G.N., M.K., B.S., and, goodness, how many more?) or
the sense in which it was used in the hallowed days of Lascelles
Hall, where everything ran in families; where you were
practically obliged to be a Lockwood, an Ambler or a Thewlis;
where, indeed, a whole eleven of Thewlises once turned out
in a match, along with a Thewlis umpire, a Thewlis scorer
and a Thewlis who took your tuppences at the gate.

I do not think there can ever have been more than one
Bosanquet, one Balaskas (X.), one Carkeek, one Dipper, one
Huish, one Pougher (pronounced Puffer), one Tarbox, or one
L. O. S. Poidevin, though if they were assembled together, you
would have the nucleus of a formidable eleven. All over the
world, there have always been lots of Browns, Joneses and
Robinsons. There have been many honourable Browns, including the stylish J.T. who, you remember, toured Australia
with Stoddart's victorious 1894-95 team and at home shared
so many first-wicket partnerships with John Tunnicliffe of
Pudsey; George of Hampshire with his carpet-bag hands, who
could bat, bowl, keep wicket, and stop a cannon-ball anywhere else in the field and was one of the few English heroes
of the ill-starred 1921 Tests; W.A. (Boy), the prolific Australian first-wicket batsman; and F.R. (Freddy), whose team's
gallant defeat in Australia in 1950-51 was nearer to victory
than the score suggests and paved the way to the recovery
and the triumph of 1954-55.

Cricket's history has had its work cut out to keep up with
the many eminent Joneses, from the ferocious Australian fast
bowler, Ernest, who bowled the notorious ball through W.G.'s

beard ('Sorry, doc, she slipped'), to Arthur O., captain of Notts and the best slip field between Tunnicliffe and Walter Hammond, and one of the most famous of all rugger referees; right down (or up) to Willie of Glamorgan, dashing left-hand bat and even more dashing, goal-dropping rugger stand-off half.

Naturally there are relays of Robinsons, from the fabulous, the legendary, the ineffable Emmott ('Thee get on wi' thi lakin', Mr. Foster, and I'll get on wi' mine'), through Ellis of that ilk, who should have gone to Australia with Hammond's team in 1946-47, to H.B., the talented and charming captain of the Canadian touring side of 1954, the only Canadian, as far as I remember, to gain an Oxford blue at cricket.

II

But, as in other walks of life, all cricketing families have to bow to the cricketing Smiths. In the oldest *Wisden* that lay near my hand—I think it was 1896—I found only a dozen Smiths. Picking up another—this time it was 1905— I found twenty-five, plus the odd Smythe; in 1939 there were fifty-four; in the current volume I counted as many as thirty-nine of them, but that is only a selection, because, as you know, of late *Wisden*, from sheer pressure of space, has had to grow a bit selective in its births and deaths.

The salient point in all this Smithery is that cricketing Smiths, like cricketing parsons, were and are a long-lived lot. The first of them was, or possibly still is, a Yorkshireman with the same initials as my own, who, unless he inconsiderately passed away in some *Wisden* that I do not possess, must now be living, probably up the dales somewhere, at the age of 107. Why not? It's a healthy county.

Mr. A. F. Smith (Camb. Univ. and Middlesex) and Mr. B. C. Smith (Northamptonshire and First Class Umpire) lived till eighty-three and C. A. Smith (Camb. Univ., Sussex and England) lived to be eighty-five. He died, full of honours, in 1948. Very possibly, as Sir Aubrey Smith, he was your favourite film star: you are bound to have seen him give some rich, vintage performances, and never a weak one among the lot. I do not suppose you ever saw him play cricket, unless you lived in Hollywood, where he was for many years the

uncrowned king of the English community, always searching
for a sound opening bat or a tricky slow bowler for his
eleven. But his more serious cricket was played a long time
before that. He was a member of the Cambridge elevens in
the four Varsity matches of 1882-85 and by his cunningly
deceptive bowling helped to bring his side victory in three of
them. In 1887-88 he was captain of one of those two English
teams touring Australia with carefree simultaneity and the
following winter he captained the first English side that made
the trip to South Africa. Only two Tests were played and
England won both far too easily. Aubrey Smith in the first
innings of the first game took five wickets for 19 but this
excellent performance was reduced to the level of the ordinary
by Johnny Briggs of Lancashire, who in the second game
had the fantastic analysis of fifteen for 29, and fourteen of
them clean bowled, at that.

Another remarkable Smith, also of Charterhouse, was G.O.,
who was in the Oxford team against Cambridge in 1895 and
'96. His name became far more illustrious in football than
in cricket. He was, like C. B. Fry, a soccer star in the ranks
of Oxford, England and the Corinthians and was probably
the most dazzling amateur centre forward in English football
history. For fifty years men would say : ' Ah, but you should
have seen G. O. Smith . . .'

G. O. Smith, as I say, did not seek renown as a cricketer
and yet, in his two Varsity matches, he performed more
doughtily than the most eminent amateur batsmen of the day.
In the two Cambridge elevens were Frank Mitchell, W. G.
Grace junior, C. J. Burnup and G. L. Jessop, while the Oxford
sides included P. F. Warner, H. K. Foster, C. B. Fry and
H. D. G. Leveson-Gower. But G. O. Smith, who had only
come into the side at the last moment, proved himself a worthy
member of such a distinguished company. In the first game he
hit up a stout-hearted not-out fifty and in the second he
carried his side to victory with a furiously hit 132, a real footballer's century.

III

Other Smiths who graced the beginning of this century
were C.L.A., a good batsman in a Sussex side rich in bat-

ting, and S. G. Smith, a versatile bat and a clever slow bowler from the West Indies, who settled in Northamptonshire and formed a sharp prong in that county's attack; W.C. (Razor), the Surrey slow bowler, always tricky and occasionally devastating. He was undoubtedly a character; once, when sent to study the form of a junior team, he was discovered in a deck-chair fast asleep. He made a useful report, all the same. Once, when umpiring at the Crystal Palace, he was so misguided as to give W.G. out, l.b.w. As the Old Man walked away, he said pityingly : ' Razor, I always thought you were a fool. Now I *know* it.' There was, too, that inspired stumper, E. J. (Tiger) Smith, now Warwickshire's genial coach, who, as we have seen, kept wicket superbly during England's triumphant Australian tour of 1911-12 (Strudwick was his understudy on this visit). The great batsmen of the side were Hobbs and Rhodes and the great bowlers F. R. Foster and Barnes, both difficult bowlers to ' take,' but Tiger took them well, partly because of his native skill and partly because he knew the bowling of Foster, his county captain, like the back of his hand.

Every August of those early years saw Yorkshire open its ranks to admit a grand Yorkshireman who kept a school at Eastbourne. This was Ernest Smith, a hard hitter, a useful slow bowler, a fine field and a fighting cricketer to whom a crisis was meat and drink. There were not many places for amateurs in the great Yorkshire sides of the period, but Ernest could force his way in.

IV

In the years between the wars there were Smiths running loose all over the place. There was a pleasant left-hander named Denis, who went in first for Derbyshire, hit the county's record number of centuries, was for a long time poised on the edge of Test honours, playing twice for England in 1935, and had far less luck in his career than so good a batsman was entitled to. A pair of Essex ' twins ' almost as renowned as Perrin and McGahey, are to be found in T.P.B. (Peter) and Ray Smith : not strictly twins, but cousins, lively all-rounders and fine fellows on and off the field. Peter made four Test appearances and did the double once; Ray has so far done the double three times, taken 100 wickets in a season seven times and three times raced to the prize for the fastest century. Another inter-war Smith was Harry, of Gloucester, (not to be confused with Tiger of Warwick), who kept wicket for England against the West Indies in 1928.

Perhaps the most colourful character among the inter-war Smiths was C.I.J. (Big Jim) Smith, the muscles of whose brawny arms were, appropriately enough, strong as iron bands. I wish that Henry Wadsworth Longfellow could have lived to see this idealised cricketing Village Blacksmith, swinging his heavy sledge with measured beat and by no means slow. It would have made his heart rejoice. A vigorous bowler and an even more vigorous bat, he made it his life's ambition to follow Albert Trott's noble example in hitting a ball over the pavilion at Lord's. He tried, in fact, to hit every ball over the pavilion and, though this beautiful ideal was not to be achieved, he was always making and breaking quick-scoring records. In 1938 against Sussex he hit 69, studded with six sixes, in twenty minutes and ten days later, off Gloucestershire's bowling, he actually hit up 66 (eight sixes)) in eighteen minutes, the first fifty of them in twelve. When bowlers saw Jim, their first inclination was to run and hide behind the sight-screen.

Big Jim, who now keeps a pub in the north, began his county career with Wiltshire. There is a tale which pictures him coming in at the end of the day when, in the last over, Wiltshire needed twelve to win. At the other end was a distinguished novelist who had not received and, as it turned out, would not receive a ball. In a non-aggressive, non-committal sort of way Jim hit the first ball over the pavilion and the second out of sight. Wiltshire is surrounded by the counties of Somerset, Dorset, Hants, Berkshire and Gloucestershire and it is not certain into which of these counties the ball had been propelled, but it had left Wiltshire for ever. As the retiring batsmen walked to the pavilion, Jim said disapprovingly, but without heat : ' Look, Mr. Balchin, you're a wicketkeeper and I'm a fast bowler, and *this* is what they make us do!'

And there was poor H. A. (Haydon) Smith, who died, all too young, half a dozen years ago. He was a tall, lanky fellow who had a useful career with Leicestershire as a fast bowler. He once took six Yorkshire wickets for a song at a time when Yorkshire could hardly be dismissed for whole oratorio. His other famous feat was more awe-inspiring; indeed, in retrospect, it makes the blood run cold. He once bowled an over of atrocious bumpers to an incoming batsman, of whose name he had not taken particular note. This was an error. The batsman was Harold Larwood.

V

As for the Smiths of today, their name, if it were not Smith, would be Legion. In the counties they are as thick as blackberries in September. Derby have an Edwin; Essex have Ray, still taking wickets and hitting more merrily than ever; Kent have a Geoffrey, who must be good because he was born in Huddersfield; Lancashire run to two at least; Sidney, a red-haired right-handed bat and Colin S., an all-rounder who bowls fast and has obtained a blue at Cambridge, where he has a namesake, D.J., to bowl at the other end. Somerset have a Roy; Sussex have a Donald, an excellent left-hand No. 1 bat, who surprised his friends in 1955 by taking quite a large number of wickets; and Leicestershire have an M.J.K.

It seems accepted in some quarters that to praise a young man is virtually to do him an injury. If this assumption is true I must, in the unlikely event of anybody's ever taking any notice of what I say, have wrought a great deal of havoc in my time. Somehow the best of our young players have survived the ordeal by laudation, and so, still protesting that I mean an obviously nice lad no evil, I will hereby state my belief that Michael J. K. Smith of Oxford University and Leicestershire may one day go in first for England in summer and play somewhere behind the scrum for England in winter.

I have a friend, a nasty-minded fellow, who swears that I can never see a good-looking gosling without shouting: ' Cygnet ! ' When he reads these lines he will growl : ' Swan-upping again . . .' But I do not care. Peter May and Colin Cowdrey are no less good because I thought them good a good long time ago. It may be that some of my cygnets will turn out to be geese after all. But if there is one true cygnet in half a dozen goslings, my picking will not be in vain.

In the Varsity match of 1954 a tall smiling fair-haired spectacled young man named M. J. K. Smith made 201 not out;

in the second innings of the 1955 game he made 104. It does
not matter that he is only the third player in the University
match to score a double hundred and a single one: he will
make more centuries yet. His scoring of over a thousand runs
in his first year at the University was a record for a freshman.
Think of all the world's great amateur batsmen who did *not*
do that. Playing for Leicestershire out of term time he made
some good scores in both these seasons. His methods are
neither original—why should they be?—nor, at first sight,
strikingly attractive to the eye: they are sound and solid,
straight and honest, without being dull. He seldom appears to
be ' hitting out ' and yet the score is pushed along at a faster
rate than by many batsmen who look more aggressive. When
I saw him in 1954 batting against Cambridge he was watchful at the beginning of the day and he was watchful at the
end, but he had made over two hundred in between and had
gone on calmly taking each ball on its merits throughout the
day. Surely this tireless concentration is the mark of a Test
player; it was certainly the mark of a young man who once
made 364.

Michael Smith is just the same in the field: vigilant, un-
fussy and supremely confident. His manner is serious but
serene, both at the wicket and holding the last line of defence
at rugger, and this unobtrusive calm is, I think, another of
the qualities which mark him out as of more than ordinary
stature. Cricket and football call for all sorts of different
qualities, but they can also be served by one or two traits
which they hold in common: an intelligent approach to the
game's problems, steadiness under pressure, a sense of anticipation which is half conscious and half instinctive, and the
appearance of having plenty of time to make the stroke or
kick. I think that Michael Smith has those qualities in plenty
and, at least in the possession of them, he reminds me of
another Smith who played cricket and rugger for Oxford and
for his country. His name? H. G. Owen-Smith, greatest of the
hyphen-Smiths, and if anybody can think of a brighter star
for wagon-hitching purposes, I should like to be put in touch
with a good astronomer.

There are, as you may remind me, numbers of half-Smiths,
such as Fellows-Smith, Oxford's lively South African, and
Knightly-Smith, the Middlesex left-hander now playing for

Gloucester. But if we embrace all the hyphen-Smiths, we shall be overcrowded.

VI

If anyone wants an eleven of all-time Smiths, I daresay we could oblige, always pre-supposing that our team are all alive, in their best form, and willing to indulge our fancy. We will have Tiger for our stumper, Big Jim and Haydon for our fast bowlers and Razor and Round-the-Corner for our slows. Michael and Denis can begin our innings, G.O. the Corinthian and Ray, the dynamic Essex all-rounder will stiffen the middle batting and Ernest, as he so often did, will come in if we play in August. Our batting order will therefore be : (1) Smith, D. (Derbyshire), (2) M. J. K. Smith (Leicestershire), (4) G. O. Smith (Oxford University), (5) Smith, R. (Essex), (6) E. Smith (Yorkshire), (7) C. A. Smith (Sussex), (8) Smith, E. J. (War-wickshire), (9) Smith, C. I. J. (Middlesex), (10) Smith, W. C. (Surrey), (11) Smith, H. A. (Leicestershire). Why have I left a vacancy at No. 3, the most vital position of all? I have reserved that post, and the captaincy might as well go with it, for the man who, when he played for Cambridge in 1892, was undoubtedly and universally known as Smith. He had another name.

It was K. S. Ranjitsinhji.

I

CHAPTER 10

THE GOLDEN YEARS

I

THE ABILITY of Surrey to win the county championship four years in succession is viewed by Yorkshiremen with respectful exasperation. The respect, which is genuine, pays due tribute to a side which has fine bowling, magnificent fielding and batting good enough to get more runs than this bowling and fielding could get most opponents out for. The exasperation arises from the fact that these are just the qualities on which Yorkshiremen have perennially prided themselves. ' Look at the averages,' they used to say. ' We've only got one batsman in the first ten, but we often have three bowlers in the first five. As for fielding, when the critics say that most English fielding is shocking, they admit they don't mean ours . . .'

Surrey's four victories in a row under a forceful captain equal and recall Yorkshire's four victories under a similarly forceful captain in 1937, 1938, 1939 and, after the break of the war, 1946. These Yorkshire sides of the thirties were powerful and there are many who say that their predecessors of the early twenties, with a bowling strength that included Rhodes, Roy Kilner, Emmott Robinson, Macaulay, Waddington and E. R. Wilson, were more powerful still. After all, they won the championship in 1919 and 1922-25. If I go further back to glance at the turn of the century, it is because the Yorkshire team of that period was not only great, but great in a great age.

Many people are now alive who as boys saw the mighty Yorkshire side who took the championship in 1900, 1901 and 1902, winning 49 matches in three seasons. At least two members of the eleven are still happily with us, one of them the most renowned of all. It is strange that *Wisden* of 1901 should say : ' Rhodes does not look by any means the most robust of players.' It could not have known that twenty-five years later he would bowl England to long-delayed victory over Australia. Certainly Wilfred Rhodes in 1900 was the leading bowler both in the county and in the country and, while in the three seasons he took 542 wickets (647 in all matches), he was perhaps even more powerful as part of a relentless attacking machine than as an individual. In 1900 it was Rhodes, Haigh and Hirst; in 1901, Rhodes Hirst and Haigh; and in 1902, Haigh, Rhodes and Hirst. Here was the three-pronged attack that batsmen of all counties learned to dread and if any one of the three needed a rest, there were reinforcements at hand in the persons of the August school-master, Ernest Smith, that rich character Ted Wainwright, and, when he returned from the South African war, F. S. Jackson. As an attack it was tremendous.

Today old gentlemen say that English fielding standards are low. It may be that I have damned iteration about fielding, but (a) it is the only sin I count for ever unpardonable and (b) I have never said that all fielding was as bad as some. In 1953 and 1955 England beat Australian teams that fielded better than themselves and the same can be said of the more recent victory over South Africa. But not all is lost. A Surrey that contains, Surridge, Stewart and Lock and a Yorkshire that has Wilson and Trueman can compete with most. If I argue that fielding is not what is was, you may retort that it never was. To prove how foolish old gentlemen can be, even (or especially) when right, let me quote from an article by D. L. A. Jephson in *Wisden* of 1901 :

'Taken as a whole the fielding has been bad, thoroughly bad. Men stand in the field today like so many "little mounds of earth," or waxen dummies in a third-rate tailor's shop. The energy, the life, the ever-watchfulness is gone, and in their place are lethargy, laziness and a wonderful yearning for rest. Today a ball is driven through two so-called fieldsmen, and instead of a simultaneous rush to gather it, the two "little mounds of earth" stand facing each other with a lingering hope in their eyes that they will not be compelled to fetch it.'

These are hard words to describe the glorious season of 1900 and Mr. Jephson in a footnote on ' mounds of earth ' says that the expression is a ' timid euphonious paraphrase ' for what he heard an old cricketer call ' clods of dirt.' I have no doubt that this in its turn was a euphemism for ' loomps of moock.' What cheers me is that the austere critic admits exceptions, both in teams and individuals. Yorkshire and Lancashire (who chased them home towards the championship) were nominated as excellent fielding sides, owing ' a large degree of success ' to their proficiency in this art.

If you know anything of the history of that brilliant period, the names of individually brilliant fieldsmen throughout the counties were those you might have expected : A. C. MacLaren, G. L. Jessop, A. O. Jones, Johnny Tyldesley for his dashing displays in the deep and Albert Trott for his pluck ' in proximity.' The fielding stars of Yorkshire's golden years were Hirst, Denton and Tunnicliffe, undoubtedly the finest mid-off, long-on and slip of the period.

Our critic of half a century ago deprecated the ' growing tendency on the part of certain fieldsmen to remove themselves as far as possible from the *dangerous* ball that travels at too great a speed.' Hirst at mid-off was absolutely fearless and this, mark you, in the day of the great classical batsmen for whom the majestic off-drive was virtually an act of religious faith. There are no fieldsmen like him now, but then there are not the off-drivers. (The last of the great mid-offs in the Hirst tradition was Arthur Gilligan.) Hirst had what is now called ' everything ': agility, anticipation, hand like jointed steel and the courage that would have attempted to stop a bullet that had already gone through a stone wall. A ball had about as much chance of getting past him as a No. 27 bus has of getting past Hammersmith Broadway.

Denton was praised, and justly so, for ' hovering on the edge of the green circle,' and cutting the batsman down to a three and even two, when he had promised himself an easy four. He had the lovely movement that seemed to blend pick-up and throw in a single graceful action. Denton's throw-in flung from any angle and pitching cleanly for the wicketkeeper to take without effort, was as accurate as Rhodes's bowling, which was as accurate as a steel precision instrument. He took many catches, for in those days there were batsmen who would time and again drive the ball hard into the long field, and, through sheer nimbleness, *made* catches which to the spectator did not seem like catches at all. It was said of him and of

Tyldesley, too, that they would dart in for catches, however impossible they might seem, rather than meekly wait to receive them first bounce.

The most renowned slip-field of the period was Tunnicliffe, though Braund ran him close and later may have been said to surpass him. Braund was famous for his swiftness of anticipation and some of his catches were spectacular in the manner we have learnt to regard as the exclusive privilege and perquisite of Godfrey Evans. Tunnicliffe's technique was less dramatic; indeed, Long John Tunnicliffe's method was similar to that of long John Langridge, who retired at the end of 1955, full of years, which he did not show, and honours, which he bore modestly. In his last season Langridge headed the list of successful fieldsmen, and departed to the wigwams of peace with a final sixty scalps at his belt. Tunnicliffe was the apostle of the unobtrusive. If you snicked a ball, you were out. That was the law and Tunnicliffe was the long arm of it. But the law was carried out without malice and certainly without ostentation.

Tunnicliffe was six feet two: his limbs were of immense length and, wherever the ball went, the Tunnicliffe hand at the end of the Tunnicliffe arm appeared to be there first. There was a horrid hypnotic touch about it. Wherever you meant the ball to go, it went scurrying just where Tunnicliffe wanted it to be. In the course of championship matches in these three seasons he held 140 catches and in his career he held 678 for Yorkshire. How hard they were few will ever know for he made virtually all of them look easy. He thought nothing of taking seven catches in a match and I cannot think that his victims thought much of it, either. He might have been played for his fielding alone but, of course, it was his batting which took him to and held him in the front rank. On the only occasion during the period when no amateur was available Tunnicliffe captained the side and captained it wisely.

The batting order of the Yorkshire side of these golden years was enough to make the boldest foeman feel thoughtful. It started with Tunnicliffe and J. T. Brown who as first-wicket batsmen were born record-breakers. In 1897 they hit 378 against Sussex and, although that record was broken shortly afterwards, in the following year against Derbyshire at Chesterfield, Tunnicliffe and Brown piled up a score of 554 which stood majestically as a record for thirty-four years until Holmes and Sutcliffe (another Pudsey man) made it take second place. It is a solemn thought that while Tunnicliffe and Brown were making their 554, Lord Hawke sat in the pavilion with his pads on for a whole day and then part of the next. A lord in waiting indeed . . .

The third man in this splendid batting order was David Denton, who, as we have seen, was a dazzler of dazzlers, and the fourth was T. L. Taylor, a stylish and forceful left-hander, who captained Cambridge, made one of the rare centuries against the Australians and, like Denton, only missed an England cap because he had to compete with Fry, Ranji, MacLaren, Spooner, Hayward, Abel, Palairet, Tyldesley and R. E. Foster. He played hockey for England and might well have played rugger for England, too, but for an injury. Today, more than half a century later, he is president of the county club and an elder statesman endowed with shrewdness and wisdom.

At the other end of the batting list came Lord Hawke, Haigh and Hunter, captain, stump-hitter and wily wicket-keeper. With a top and tail of that quality there was no weakening in the middle, for there you would see the three men who are, in my unaggressive opinion, the three greatest all-rounders who ever handled bat and ball : Hirst, Rhodes and F. S. Jackson. Players who turned out less frequently and over certain periods filled the odd place in the team were men whom any county would have been glad to have : Frank Mitchell, Ernest Smith, Ted Wainwright and Lees Whitehead, the last of whom came very near to the top of the first class batting averages in 1900. Of the great players of the period at least ten were honoured as ‘ cricketers of the year.’ David Hunter was the only regular Yorkshireman of the period who was not so honoured, but this is no criticism of David, who was generally recognised as second to Lilley, as Denton was second to Tyldesley. The reason for Hunter’s seeming neglect is merely that the standards of wicketkeeping have always been high and nobody says thank you for a job uniformly well done.

Nobody can say that this conquering side enjoyed easy conquests. A mere glance at a few of the contemporary counties

shows that victory had to be fought for all the way. Some
sides had a wealth of batting. Lancashire began with A. C.
MacLaren, R. H. Spooner and Tyldesley, an even more
powerful initial trio than Yorkshire's. Surrey had Abel, Hayward and Lockwood, Sussex had C. B. Fry and K. S. Ranjitsinhji, and Gloucestershire, who had recently lost Grace, had
G. L. Jessop and C. L. Townsend, and even the modest
Hampshire could at times call on that most remarkable of
military cricketers, Major R. M. Poore. Somebody some day
will set down an adequate account of the achievements of
this soldier-cricketer, whom even *Wisden* called sensational,
and everybody else will be surprised.

Every county had its bowlers of quality. There were fast
ones like Mold, W. M. Bradley, Wass and Richardson and
slow ones like Colin Blythe, Walter Mead and Johnny Briggs,
drawing near to the sad end of his career but still bowling
with his old cunning. The greatest of the mediums was Albert
Trott, who took 211 wickets in 1900 and was described as
' inventive, versatile and inexhaustible in resource.'

Against opposition of this strength Yorkshire played even
more strongly. Hirst in the three years made 3,772 runs and
Rhodes took 542 wickets. He was the first bowler to take
200 wickets in a county season. (Appleyard, fifty-one years
later, took 200 wickets in his *first* season.) Several victories
were won by an innings in one day or its equivalent in hours
in a wet summer. There were times when this almost became
a habit.

In the first game in 1900, for instance, the aggregate
for the whole match was less than two hundred and many
years must have passed before there was another game where
a side failed to get a hundred and won by an innings. (The
present Surrey side have come nearer to the habit.) There was
an almost similar result in the 1901 match at Leyton. The
game was not quite finished on the first day, but it went a
long way : twenty-seven wickets fell by six-thirty and the rest
took less than an hour to dispose of the next morning. Essex
made only 71 runs in their two innings and Yorkshire, who
had only just topped the hundred, won by an innings and 33.
Hirst's match figures were twelve for 29. In the same season
Yorkshire caught Notts on what must have been a fiendish
wicket, Rhodes ran riot and in forty-seven balls took six

wickets for 4 runs. Haigh did not do so well, merely getting
four for 8.

The Roses match of 1902 was another of these struggles in
which ball conquered bat. Although Yorkshire could make
only 148 (40 for the last two wickets), they dismissed Lancashire twice for 126. And that Lancashire eleven contained
MacLaren, Tyldesley, Albert Ward and James Hallows. A
fourth example was Yorkshire's game at Bradford with Middlesex when 175 was enough to secure an innings victory.
You never knew which Yorkshire bowler, besides Rhodes,
would suddenly ' go mad.' In the first innings Rhodes took
seven for 24. In the second it was Haigh's turn to take seven.

The summer of 1902 was one of those maddening seasons
when evil weather was king, when far too many games were
ruined by rain and slow bowlers made hay of their opponents
as soon as the sun shone. Yorkshire won their third successive
championship and won it deservedly, in spite of, perhaps even
because of, demands for Test needs on their best players.
They won, as Surrey won in 1955, by their almost infinite
ability to bring out able reserves who played like seasoned old-
timers. In this season of the tenth Australian visit the English
Test sides needed, and were able to claim, a hard core of
Yorkshiremen : Rhodes and Jackson played in five Tests;
Hirst played in four and Haigh and Taylor were included in
' selected ' twelves. This is a noble proportion but, somewhat
grudgingly, I feel it should have been even larger. Though
England were immensely strong, Australia won the rubber
and for this unhappy outcome there were two reasons.

One was that in the Birmingham game rain saved the
Australians from inevitable defeat after Hirst and Rhodes
had dismissed them for 36 (Hirst three for 15, Rhodes seven
for 17). The other was the loss of the Manchester game by
three runs : a defeat which might reasonably have been
avoided if either Hirst or Haigh had been picked instead of
that excellent county bowler, Fred Tate. It is over half a century ago, but the misfortunes of poor Fred in this game have
become almost as inevitable a part of our comical-tragical
literature as those of Moses Primrose. They have been enshrined not merely in Cardus's brilliant prose but in a radio
interview which Len Braund, one of the game's two survivors,*

* It is sad to record that Braund died earlier this year.

gave to John Arlott. That broadcast was at once one of the most poignant, fascinating and funny bits of comedy that ever came over the air. There was an almost classic touch in Braund's description of Tate's final discomfiture : ' Down went Fred's castle.' And there was a world of dramatic irony in Braund's attempt to comfort his sorrowing friend : ' Cheer up, Fred, they'll forget it in a week.' It has not been forgotten in nearly three thousand weeks.

It seems plain enough that Haigh should have been in the twelve and Hirst should indubitably have been in the eleven. I base my judgment, not on wisdom fifty-four years after the event, but on the apocalyptic denunciations of the selectors by Uncle Walter, an essentially kind-hearted man. He even blamed Lord Hawke who, for him, could normally do no wrong. Uncle Walter said that Haigh was not picked because Lord Hawke would not allow Yorkshire to play its county match at Worcester with its four best players missing and MacLaren, he said, left out Hirst on the morning of the match, just to *larn* Lord Hawke what would happen. It was the only outrageous thing I ever heard Uncle Walter say. He was suffering under great emotional stress.

The following week at Headingley, Yorkshire bowlers once more demanded credence for the incredible. Hirst and Rhodes had put the Australians out for 36. Now Hirst (five for 9) and Jackson (five for 12) put them out for 23. This remains, as well it might, the most shattering defeat, the most inhospitable treatment ever inflicted on England's cricketing guests.

Here were the heroes, conquering and unconquerable. Not quite unconquerable. For an account of the strange events which led to this dramatic change of fortune, as the old novelists used to say, we must wait for another chapter.

CHAPTER 11

HOW TO WIN CHAMPIONSHIPS

I

IT IS a firm parliamentary custom for a speaker on a controversial subject to declare his interest and, as the county championship is a highly controversial question, I will, to no one's surprise at this stage, declare myself a Yorkshireman, at least for the purposes of argument. At once several questions arise. Who have won the championship most often? Who holds the championship now? Who are likeliest to win it in the future? And what are the qualities that make a championship side?

Everybody knows the answers to the first two questions. They are historical and statistical. Yorkshire are not averse from mentioning their twenty-two victories, plus a half-share in 1949, though they may feel rather pensively in the manner of the governors of North and South Carolina, that it is now a long time between championships. Surrey have no need to be modest about their successive triumphs in the last four years, and if anyone doubts Surrey's claim to have richly deserved these honours, I reckon his judgment of cricketing merit to be at fault. As for the other two questions, they cannot be answered at once by concrete facts and figures. Nobody knows, though almost everybody would attempt to give an answer, based on varying degrees of loyalty, local patriotism, pious hope and wishful thinking. The one thing that is dead certain is that nobody *knows* for certain.

But at least a passing glance can be cast upon some of the sides who in the past have carried off the prizes with such distinction and, indeed, sometimes with a kind of arrogance. *Wisdens,* if you have enough of them, will show many parallels between the great Yorkshire side at the turn of the century and Surridge's Surrey (1952, '53, '54, '55 and ?). There were other outstanding Yorkshire sides, like those of the early nineteen-twenties which were manned by the most formidable, even ferocious, bunch of bowlers any county ever had, and those of the thirties which, as we have seen, enjoyed the incomparable leadership of Brian Sellers. There were those three memorable Lancashire years of 1926, '27 and '28, with Ernest Tyldesley in his heyday, and Macdonald (fast), Richard Tyldesley (slow) and Cecil Parkin (funny), capable of bowling practically everybody in sight. There were the sparkling and nearly unconquerable Kentish elevens of round about 1909, of which the glorious Frank Woolley was an ordinary member! (It is a quaint parallel that Sir Winston Churchill was at that time an ordinary member of a brilliant Cabinet.) And there was that 1947 Middlesex side with its gargantuan scoring powers, when Compton and Edrich ran riot and all the other counties' bowlers practically lay down and died. There have been very fine Notts sides; once there was Glamorgan, once Derby, twice there was Warwick and in 1955 Hampshire came up into a place in an exciting final gallop.

II

What then makes a winning side? What qualities did these teams possess, not owned by the others? I once listened respectfully to a snatch of radio dialogue.

Interlocutor: ' They tell me, sir, you were a great captain. Is that so?'

C. B. Fry (with just a hint in his voice that he has not yet learnt to suffer fools gladly): ' Of course I was a great captain. *I had great bowlers.*'

Now this, I think, is the first dependable principle. Not only does the aphorism come from C. B. Fry, who is probably —and this is only one of his attributes—the finest all-round athlete England has ever bred. It is true in its own right. All the conquering sides had outstanding bowlers (and have you noticed how important it seems to be to have a good slow left-hander?) whether it was Yorkshire's earlier Hirst, Rhodes and Haigh or later Bowes and Verity or that battling battalion that came in between with Macaulay, Waddington, Emmott Robinson, Roy Kilner, E. R. Wilson and Rhodes, who was already a veteran but was to go on being a veteran for another ten years yet.

The modern side most easily comparable with these York-shire bowling sides is Surrey's hostile attack, led by the famous L-formation of Lock, Laker and Loader with Alec Bedser in close support, not to mention Surridge who could easily take a good many more wickets than he does, if his other bowlers did not save him the trouble. Just as in 1954 and '55 Brian Close might well have taken more wickets if Appleyard, True-man and Wardle had not taken them first. Even the Middle-sex of 1947, with their astronomical scores, could not have crowned themselves with laurels if their batsmen had not been backed by the sterling work of Jack Young, Laurie Gray and Jim Sims, the last of whom was by that time almost an ever-green laurel himself.

The next thing to great bowling is great fielding and par-ticuarly close-to-the-wicket fielding. I am not naturally dog-matic, partly because I hate quarrelling, and partly because, as a wise and noble mind once discovered, the world is so full of a number of things. But I would again and again cry the importance of fielding to the four winds of heaven. The old Yorkshire sides were ardent fieldsmen as a matter of course, if not as a matter of religion. When John Tunnicliffe was in the slips, it must have seemed to the slightly mesmerised bats-man that there were at least three men lying in ambush for him. My Uncle Walter, who saw Tunnicliffe in his prime, said he had as many arms as a hat-rack. Now that batting and bowling patterns have changed a good deal and ticklings round the corner are seen more frequently than straight drives over the bowler's head, the setting of the modern field looks a little odd to the old-fashioned spectator. It must appear too, a little uncomfortable to the batsman, who sees himself hemmed in and beleaguered by slips, leg-slips, silly mid-offs, silly mid-ons and whole shoals of short-legs and even silly gullies crouching round him like terriers waiting for the last rat to run out of the base of the haystack at threshing time. There are some batsmen who are not intimidated by this sort of thing. It does not intimidate the very best young bats-men, like May or Cowdrey, but I have seen whole teams ' worried out' by aggressive fielding of this kind, which can become a veritable war of nerves.

In the thirties, as we have noted, you would see Brian Sellers leading out his team and instantly exercising a kind of dominance over the batsmen. The pirates were in command and their victim, the batsman, walked the plank. And even if he momentarily survived, he must have felt like a poor swimmer in shark-infested waters. As for the present Surrey side in the field, their motto is : ' Escape me never !' If a ball flies wide of Barrington it will not get past Stewart; if it passes Lock—and this can only be a miracle if it does—it will not pass Surridge. What an inspired lot of pocket-pickers and artful dodgers those Surrey close-fieldsmen would have made if they had chosen a different profession. Fagin would have had practically nothing to teach them.

The third element is vital captaincy, and we have already glanced at some gallant captains. About captaincy no more need be said here than that it is for obvious reasons more difficult than it used to be, but that integrity of character, in conjunction with courtesy and good sportsmanship, is still the quality that conquers all.

There is one more thing. When Yorkshire won the championship in the golden years, they lost only two matches, both of them to Somerset, and when Middlesex ran out victors in 1947, they also lowered their colours to Somerset, in what should be called Tremlett's match, one of the most exciting games I ever saw. And there have been others in between.

So the recipe is easy. You can win the championship by great bowling, keen in-fielding, dynamic captaincy, and getting beaten by Somerset.

It seems a little hard on Somerset.

V

Not that Somerset have ever complained. They have had their downs, but their ups are something to boast of. Their win in 1947 over Middlesex was over the most prolific batting side of modern times and the great Yorkshire team whom they defeated twice was probably the most powerful combination that ever represented a county. I do not discount for a moment the present powerful Surrey side, but I think that half a century ago the opposition was stiffer.

At the bottom of the table stood Somerset. They seemed made, as they sometimes seemed in more recent years, the whipping boys of all the world. Against ordinary sides, Somerset played their ordinary best, and this best was seldom good enough. But when they came to grips with their alleged betters, they pulled out of the bag a better best than they had ever been known to possess before. It was magnificent, but was it cricket? Indeed it was : cricket of the most enthralling kind.

When Somerset failed, there was no secret about the reason. They had some remarkable players—and there have been few more remarkable players than Palairet, Braund and Sammy Woods—but they were seldom able to place a reliable first eleven in the field at a given time. Sammy Woods laid his finger on the spot when he was heard at a later date to complain : ' Lord Hawke could write down the names of a dozen players on the first of May and on the first of August they would still be playing together. But by the first of August I should have had about three times as many names on my list, and never a real eleven.'

Nevertheless, in their matches against Yorkshire, they made a special effort to get a talented side together. Greek met Greek, sparks flew and fireworks went off almost automatically. In the 1901 match at Taunton excitement kept on mounting in a wave until, after a jewelled century by Palairet and characteristic nineties by T. L. Taylor on one side and Sammy Woods on the other, Yorkshire with six wickets down in their second innings still needed 122 to win. Wainwright and his captain, with a stubborn backs-to-the-wall effort, dragged the game slowly round, but when David Hunter came down the steps at twenty-seven minutes past six, there were two runs between Yorkshire and victory and one wicket between Yorkshire and possible defeat. Rhodes, a slender young man but all steel in a crisis, took a single. Then Hunter hit a two and the champions, after the fright of their lives, had won by one wicket.

In the return game at Headingley there was at first no hint of drama to come. Rhodes, Hirst and Haigh tumbled Somerset out for a mere 87, of which more than half was violently hammered out by Sammy Woods. Yorkshire, after a slightly palsied start, ran out well over 200 runs ahead and, oddly enough, it was also Rhodes, Hirst and Haigh who were responsible for the bulk of the runs.

With the second innings came the gaiety, but not for Yorkshire. Palairet and Braund set off at a furious pace and knocked off the deficit almost insolently. There can never have been, before or since, a more beautiful player to watch than L. C. H. Palairet, who was the batsmen's batsman as surely as Edmund Spenser was the poets' poet. In his style the perfection of poise and grace was enshrined for ever. That day he made 173 runs and every one came from a stroke that was a thing of beauty. Nor was he the only thorn in York-shire's flesh. Braund was the finest all-rounder in cricket's golden age, always except three Yorkshiremen, and perhaps, but for another Yorkshireman, Tunnicliffe, the world's best slip field. That day Braund reached the heights and treated the bemused Headingley spectators to a hundred that was pulsing with life and colour. F. A. Phillips, by no means such a superlative batsman as Palairet or Braund, also contributed a century and then the irrepressible Sammy Woods and V. T. Hill trampled on the mangled remains of the Yorkshire bowl-ing with fifty apiece. It was, as Sammy said, taking candy from a child. The demoralisation of the Yorkshire attack may be gauged by the appalling fact that Hirst took one wicket for 189. Batsmen had to pay for that for years afterwards. Hirst was the last person in the world to bear malice : it was a matter of re-establishing self-respect.

So quickly had Somerset amassed their monumental total that there was time to set Yorkshire nearly 400 to win and get them out for less. Yorkshire were not so much defeated as demolished.

I do not know if Yorkshire's defeat at Sheffield the follow-ing year should be considered as a greater or lesser tragedy. In the Leeds game the Yorkshire bowling had been collared and soundly cuffed; at Sheffield, on the contrary, the York-shire bowlers were superb. On the first day Jackson, home from less pleasant duties in South Africa, took six wickets for 29; on the second the magnificent Schofield Haigh had one of his bouts of sheer unplayableness, striking the stumps time after time—six for 19, five of them clean bowled. *And York-shire lost.*

They lost because no Yorkshire batsman managed to face that attack as boldly as did that fatal pair, Palairet and Braund. In each innings these two made well over half their side's score. Braund had a match that normally could only have happened in a romantic schoolboy's dreams. His was the top score in each innings and he received very little help from any of his comrades except Palairet. There was one battering burst from Gill, but the rest was pathos. In Yorkshire's first innings Braund took six for 30. After that came Haigh's stump-hitting outburst, and then Yorkshire were left with the modest total of 119 to make.

Their failure was absolute. At 16 Cranfield had J. T. Brown caught in the slips and then Braund began to take his grip. If you were to look at the score-sheet, you might almost imagine that he was operating at both ends. Sometimes his leg-breaks hit the stumps and sometimes they beat both bat and wicket and earned their victims a stumping. The left-hander, T. L. Taylor, batted with polished obstinacy for 18, and for the ninth wicket Rhodes and Lord Hawke put on 11; it was one of the best stands of the match. But Braund took every other wicket, finishing off with nine for 41, and Yorkshire lost by 34 runs.

These two defeats left their mark on the champions for years, and long afterwards, when West Riding babies were unduly troublesome, fratching and tewing in their mothers' arms, West Riding mothers would say: 'You 'oosh, or Len Braund will come and get you . . .'

This happened over fifty years ago. All may reasonably be forgiven and to the small band of survivors of those heroic encounters, not least to Leonard Braund himself, we can at least wish many hours of bright evening sunshine.

CHAPTER 12

DON'T SHOOT!

I

MY TALENTED fellow-countryman, Robert Burns, once exclaimed in a rare moment of exasperation: 'Damn the frigid pedant soul of criticism for ever and ever!' This seems a moderate and reasonable imprecation. It is not the snarl of a sourpuss, but a cry from a warm-hearted soul who loved his fellow men. I hate criticism. You hate criticism. We all hate criticism, and yet, here is the paradox: when we criticise critics (blast them), we become critics ourselves. I desire to criticise three particular kinds of critic: those who criticise selectors, those who criticise cricket-writers and those who criticise all-rounders.

II

Don't shoot the selectors! We all do it. I even do it myself, like many a better man, while shouting shrilly for tolerance and goodwill. I have even repeated, in dignified tones, Uncle Walter's assertion that a grave error was committed when Jessop and Hirst were left out of the Manchester Test of 1902. But, even allowing for partisanship, which is necessary (within reason), and for prejudice, which is reasonable (up to a point), I feel that a defence may be put up for even so friendless a body as Test selectors.

We tend to treat them as we treat the leaders of the political parties to which we do not belong: that is, through a remarkable form of schizophrenia, they are gifted simultaneously with diabolical cunning and bone-headed stupidity. They are completely ignorant of the elements of the game of cricket and at the same time full of clever tricks designed to sabotage the national effort and keep obvious England players from our county out of the team. They blatantly favour men

K   145

from their own counties and are blindly prejudiced in favour of north or south, as the case may be. They are deaf to our disinterested advice. They do not pick the right eleven, even when we have helped by giving them the names of at least eighteen indispensables, the absence of any single one of whom would lead to disaster.

Every side that leaves these shores is the weakest that ever sailed, especially those that are so misguided as eventually to win the rubber. If we win we win, but if we lose, it is the selectors' fault. In 1955 when England and South Africa had won two Tests each we had tipped South Africa to win the fifth; at least, we were ready with our blame for the inevitable defeat. Where, we asked, was the magnificent combination that had retained the Ashes the winter before? (We had called it anything but that when it went out.) Now the winning team was no more and it was the selectors' fault. They were personally responsible for Hutton's discs, Compton's knee, Tyson's heel, Evans's and Cowdrey's fingers, Statham's stomach, and injuries to Appleyard. As sabotage, this must have been fairly comprehensive. They were wrong to play Bailey. They were wrong to drop Bailey. They were wrong to bring Bailey in again. They were wrong . . .

Let me be eccentric and take on the role of devil's advocate for, if selectors are not devils, who are? Let me postulate something utterly naïve: first, that the selectors, whoever they are and in whichever season they function, are at least as wishful for victory as we are and are just as keen to pick a team that would bring victory home. Furthermore, they may even know more than we do about the players, their attainments, and the state of their discs, fingers, toes, heels, knees and their temperaments. In fact, they do the job more keenly, more intelligently and more efficiently than their critics, even their newspaper critics, are ever likely to do.

III

Don't shoot the cricket writer. At least, don't shoot them all; at any rate, not all at once. There are, we are all agreed, too many cricket books. But then, as any publisher will tell you, there are too many books, period. Everybody, it appears, wants to write about cricket, whether anybody wants to read about cricket or not. Some of the books are good, some are bad and many are indifferent, but why, since this classification applies equally to all human beings, institutions and activities, need it be regarded as a final condemnation?

I once was a member of a brains trust, as it is laughingly called, and was asked for the names of the best ten cricket books. Without thinking, which is the way with brains trusts, I replied: 'One, Nyren, two Altham, and three, any eight of Cardus.' Even when I have had time to think, I do not wish to change that opinion. *The Young Cricketer's Tutor,* which John Nyren published in 1833, tells the early history of the Hambledon club, 'though 'tis fifty years bygone,' and is as much a classic of the England language as, say, *The Vicar of Wakefield* which treats of broadly the same period. The Hambledon men are the heroes of the club which, though not the oldest, was the most illustrious in cricket history. Its richest period was the second half of the eighteenth century and a true background of Hambledon would be an illuminated page from the history of England's green and pleasant land. 'Little Hambledon pitted against all England was a proud thought for Hampshire . . .' I would no more bother to praise Nyren than to patronise Chaucer, for, judged in another sense, Hambledon plays something of the same part in English cricket as Chaucer in English literature and there is a true Englishness, rich and deep and strong, that links Nyren's cricketers with Chaucer's pilgrims, though six centuries may have rolled between them.

By Altham I mean *A History of Cricket* by H. S. Altham, the current edition being by H. S. Altham and E. W. Swanton; a massive record of the game from first beginnings out to the undiscovered ends, written with authority and affection, accuracy and charm—virtues that are by no means commonly found in each other's company, all between the covers of one book. As for Cardus, he is the great cricket-writer as surely as Grace was the great cricketer; he is as elegant a stylist as his admired R. H. Spooner, and everything he writes has a touch of enchantment.

The great mass of other books are either tour-books or auto-biographies. The tour-book as a form of expression has grown from a delicate seedling to a dense undergrowth; on the last two tours to Australia practically every living English writer except Dame Edith Sitwell has written a book and, concerning tour-books in general (the best of which, between *Wickets in the West* and *Australia 55,* are admittedly splendid) one is tempted to echo the cry of the poet Longfellow : ' Beware the awful avalanche.' Of the autobiography you can say, as Harry Tate said of cheese : ' There's nothing like it and, if it's bad, *then* there's nothing like it.' There never was a genre that varied so widely. Why, some of the chaps even wrote them themselves. And very nearly the wittiest thing I have ever read on cricket, or any other subject, is Douglas Insole's delightful introduction to Trevor Bailey's *Playing to Win.*

But the writers whom cricketers want to shoot are not the writers of cricket books. This view is less flattering than it sounds, for such tolerance is based on the belief that nobody reads books, anyhow. For most cricketers a writer is a man who writes about current cricket for a newspaper and I have sometimes seen honest cricketers, otherwise the most tolerant and balanced of men, go almost black in the face when the subject crops up. There are some writers whom cricketers view with an amiably scornful tolerance and some who positively set their teeth on edge.

Is there any defence? There is always *some* defence. Even the inveterate offender is given a chance. We are a humane people. Capital punishment is restricted to convicted murderers and pedestrians and the murderers will have a fair trial. Is not the newspaperman entitled to as equitable a hearing? I have an instinctive and painful—actually physically painful sympathy with a cricketer who is being barracked by the ignorant in the stands or the supercilious in the newspapers. When in 1955 I heard Trevor Bailey being given the slow handclap for what was in fact a courageous and necessary defensive effort, I felt outraged. But Bailey did not, and for that reason, if for no other, I would play him in a Test side, because of this obvious force of character.

Nevertheless, while no one should get hot under the collar about intelligent and friendly criticism, sympathy is due to the man who is doing the job and not to the barracker. But the argument, like so many honest arguments, works both ways. The newspaperman is also doing a job and some of them do the job remarkably well. To my cricketer-friends I think I should say : ' Try all the newspapers in turn, for a week, if you can bear it. You will soon learn which newspapers and which newspapermen do the job properly. Stick to those newspapers and leave the others alone.'

It is an odd thing that cricketers and cricket-lovers often complain of the unfairness of the Press, as if there actually was a single horrid thing called the Press. It is absurd to include, say, *The Manchester Guardian* or *The Daily Telegraph* in one lump with *The Daily Plonk* under the title of the Press. You might just as well designate Markova and Narkover under the indivisible heading of culture. There is no such thing as the Press: only newspapers. It is best to support a paper whose cricket comments are fair and sensible. I agree that there are sports writers whose comments are neither fair nor sensible. I cannot think why. I know what they say when they are asked why they write as they do. They say: ' That's what my editor wants.' Or: ' That's what the public like.' Editors are strange creatures and have as many strange fancies as expectant mothers, but I cannot think that the part of the public which loves cricket likes or wants anything of the sort. What puzzles me is why this sort of paper bothers to give any cricket news at all. Nevertheless, the very mixed body of people known as the cricket public have the remedy in their own hands. Let them drop the newspapers whose cricket is done ignorantly, tastelessly and unfairly, and cherish those whose cricket is done well. And don't shoot the fellow who is trying to do it.

IV

Don't shoot the all-rounder. I do not know who first had a bad word for the all-rounder—some say it was the irreverent Bill O'Reilly—but nowadays nobody has a good one. The ability both to bat and bowl has become, like property-owning, almost a criminal offence. So unreasonable is the modern prejudice against the all-rounder that batsmen who can bowl and bowlers who can bat seldom admit the fact. It may be used in evidence against them. Word would seem to have gone forth from some critical Sinai that a side which can bat down to No. 6 has something unhealthy about it and if anybody below No. 5 is capable of making double figures he ought to be escorted off the pitch by disapproving police.

Were all-rounders always a ' bad ' thing or have they only recently become so? Why is it reckoned wrong to have in your eleven a cricketer of the quality of Keith Miller who by a single feat of either batting or bowling might win a match single-handed? Or, speaking more modestly and looking nearer home, what is the matter with a type like Trevor Bailey, whose batting in England in 1953 and 1955 and bowling in the West Indies in 1953-54 changed the fate of several games? Did our South African visitors of 1955 suffer seriously because their first-wicket batsman, Trevor Goddard, was also one of their most penetrative bowlers?

The greatest of cricket-writers has adjured the cricket world to return to first principles. For me first principles enshrine the golden years at the turn of the century when all-rounders were the life's blood of every county side. Consider, even if the matter is merely of academic and historic interest, the England eleven which was robbed of victory by rain at Birmingham in 1902. Those whose judgment is to be respected reckoned this eleven to be the best that ever walked on to a field. It contained Hirst, Rhodes and Jackson, whom I would designate as the three greatest all-rounders in cricket history. (This is a dogmatic statement, but the pre-eminence of these three is for me virtually a first principle.) Not merely did this eleven contain the three shining ones, it had G. L. Jessop, Braund and Lockwood as well. The greatest eleven had six all-rounders, all tremendous fellows, and now, in this less glorious age, we boggle at employing one.

Is there not always room in an England side for men of that calibre? Nor is there the slightest reason, just to please me to go back half a century. Look down the list in your current *Wisden* of cricketers who have achieved the double. Leaving aside Hirst (14) and Rhodes (16), would you not rush to pick somebody as good as, say, J. W. H. T. Douglas, Maurice Tate or George Geary if you had a choice? While you recall that Hammond was the dominating batsman of his era, do not forget that he took 85 wickets in Test matches, a figure not achieved by many specialist bowlers. Woolley was undoubtedly the most attractive left-hand batsman who ever played for England, but he was a bowler, too. In the first Test match I ever saw—it was against the Australians at the Oval in 1912—he took five wickets in each innings and, over the whole game, enjoyed considerably greater success than the gentleman at the other end, who merely happened to be Sidney Barnes, the best bowler of that, or perhaps, any period. The earliest triumphs of the mercurial Macartney were with the ball rather than with the bat.

I find it hard to believe that these outstanding players should now be considered retrospectively unworthy of their salt. The argument might be on a little firmer ground if it were based on a temporary dearth of first-class all-rounders; that is, if the objection were couched in some such terms as : ' We would play all-rounders if there were any good enough, but unfortunately . . .'

Whether or not this is valid at a given time, it should not be accepted as a permanent rule. If there were no such thing as an all-rounder I contend that, as Voltáire said of the Deity, it would be necessary to invent him; at any rate, it is treason to cricket to discourage him for discouragement's sake. If it is considered right to discourage all-rounders during a lean period, has it also been considered where that argument will eventually lead? There have been lean times for others than all-rounders. Until the glorious emergence of Tyson, Statham, Trueman and Appleyard. there was indeed a lean time for bowlers in the England side, and for years after the war we beheld the heroic spectacle of Alec Bedser (bless his great heart) bowling for England to all intents and purposes at both ends. Did we then say that bowlers were a mistake and that we should concentrate on running the batsmen out? No. More seriously than ever we had tried before, we went out into the highways and byways to find bowlers and, by the mercy of providence, bowlers were found.

For years England's batting lay under a cloud : first Compton, then Hutton, bore the burden almost alone. It was Louis XV who said : ' *Après moi le déluge!*' Compton in 1948 and Hutton for several years afterwards might well have exclaimed : ' After me the washout . . .' Then we were fortunate enough to find May and Cowdrey, for whom we should thank heaven, fasting, with at least a word of thanks to the selectors who picked them. But even now England are hardly out of the wood; a pessimist might growl that we still hardly bat down to No. 6 with an unhappy gap at No. 2, anyway. But because of these difficulties, we do not argue that the

search for batsmen should be given up. We still sensibly keep
an eye on promising young batsmen, such as Barrington,
Parks, Peter Richardson and Michael Smith. If we still
honour bowlers and batsmen, why are we so prejudiced
against bowler-batsmen?

The greatest cricketer of all time, the Champion himself,
was an all-rounder. Cricket, like other 'best' things in life,
has its roots in versatility, diversity and infinite variety. All-
rounders of the breed of Noble, Armstrong, Jack Gregory,
Faulkner and the irrepressible Constantine have added immeasurably to its riches throughout the Commonwealth. I have
sometimes thought that Constantine, such was his quicksilver
quality, would have liked to bat with one hand and bowl with
the other. Furthermore, the players most patently valuable to
their county sides are men skilled alike in batting, bowling
and fielding such as Dooland, Tribe, Goonesena and Marshall,
the last of whom played a leading part in his county's rise
to eminence in 1955. None of these fine all-rounders may play
for England, more's the pity.

The lively captaincy of Wooller, Yardley and Palmer has
never suffered from the fact that they are all-rounders; indeed,
it gains much and loses nothing.

I am making no plea that every lad who can bowl a bit
and bat a bit should be flung into a Test team. People who
are mediocre performers in two departments are, of course,
not all-rounders. An authority to whom I would always defer
has said that the 1954-55 Tests were won by specialists. That,
in its context, is a fact, but, with deep respect, it is not in
itself a policy. If it were it would mean going into battle with
two batsmen, two bowlers and a wicket-keeper. I am even
worried—you say it is merely my age—about the word, specialist. I could denote the very highest quality, a Bradman, an
O'Reilly, an Oldfield. I accept the term at that level. But so
often, off as well as on the field, a specialist is merely a man
who cannot do anything else. It is impossible to admire that
kind of specialist. If the word is going to mean anything at all,
it should have a wider content. Was George Hirst a specialist?
Yes. He was a specialist in batting, bowling and fielding. Is
Keith Miller a specialist? He is a specialist not only in batting, bowling and fielding, but in a match-winning quality of
his own.

Even when specialists are unimpeachably true specialists, like May, Cowdrey, Tyson, Statham and Evans, this is not enough, because a cricket team should consist of eleven men. I agree that if you cannot win with five bowlers you cannot win with more but, on the other hand, I do not think you can guarantee to go on winning with only two batsmen. Even if you have five specialist batsman, your score does not look very pretty if it virtually stops dead after No. 5. The answer is that having got your specialists (and may heaven be praised for all five of them), you must build up the rest of your eleven. Without waving too many flags, or advertising too many swans among the goslings, it should be possible to keep an eye on the talented youngsters within reach who are, in fact, the next lot after Close, Titmus, Bennett, Sainsbury, and one or two others. Such material is as precious as rubies. It would be a pity to throw it away.

CHAPTER 13

HOODOO AT HEADINGLEY

I

LEEDS IS not a sinister name and Headingley is even less forbidding, but there have been times when, for England struggling against friendly but mortal foes, the very word is like a knell. As Uncle Walter said, something funny was always happening there, and when he said *funny,* the vowel was as broad as Maurice Leyland's bat. Headingley is a pleasant ground, not as rural as Worcester but by no means as urban as Bramall Lane. It has a running track round the boundary, a slightly disconcerting slope from north to south in the playing area, and the Rugby League ground at its back to keep it cosy in winter. Headingley has earned its right to a regular Test match by the accommodation it can offer : it can seat over 30,000 bodies comfortably and, in addition, many more enthusiastic souls who (rightly enough) are more interested in cricket than in mere bodily comfort. It has also been for many years the home of that incubator of so much that is noblest and best in Yorkshire and England cricket, the winter shed, so long and lovingly presided over by George Hirst and on which, I like to think, that serene spirit still gazes benignly down.

In the old days when only three Tests were played, games were allotted to Lord's, the Oval and Old Trafford, but in 1899, when the number was increased to five, Leeds was given its chance. The first match was a bowlers' match which England might have won but for the little devil of ill-luck which made its first appearance then and has never completely disappeared. In a low-scoring first innings England led by 48 runs and at the end of the second day had knocked off 19 for no wicket of the 177 they required to win. It rained all night and play was impossible on the third day.

The game was unlucky not merely because England were

robbed by the weather of almost certain victory but because
it was here that poor Johnny Briggs, that irrepressible all-
rounder and gay skip-jack of a man, suffered a serious mental breakdown. Actually he played a few times for Lancashire
the following year, but after a further breakdown, he was
unable to play any more and eventually carried off to an
asylum. It has been said that he was not unhappy and that he
spent his time under the delusion that he was successfully
bowling out the Australians, but on the whole *Wisden's* words
give the true picture: ' It was a sad end to a very brilliant
career . . .'

The 1902 Australian match which might have been played
at Leeds was given to Sheffield where, incidentally, England
took a heavy beating, and the next Headingley Test was in
1905. This was the glorious year in which F. S. Jackson captained England, won the toss five times and topped the
batting and bowling averages. There was a captain, if you
like, and there, too, was an unanswerable argument for the
encouragement of the all-rounder. But even under the inspiration of the mighty Jackson, England only drew the Leeds
game. They won at Trent Bridge and Old Trafford, so that
the Ashes were happily retained, but at Leeds the Australians
were able to stage a strategic retreat and England failed to
dislodge them in time.

Up to a point it was a magnificent game. England made a
shaky start on a horrid wicket and only a supreme captain's
effort of 144 not out by Jackson brought them back from the
brink of disaster. England had as varied an attack as has ever
taken the field, consisting of Blythe (slow), Bosanquet (googly),
Haigh (medium), Jackson (medium fast), Hirst (fast), and
Warren of Derbyshire (very fast). It was Warren who did the
most serious damage and Australia finished their first innings
over a hundred behind. England's obvious duty from that
moment was to go for the runs, pile up a useful score as
speedily as possible and then give the Australians the worst of
whatever was going on the third day. (Remember that in
those days most cricketers were so reactionary and ignorant
as to try to finish a Test match, like any other match, in
three days.)

But England were not allowed to force their way into a
winning position, for although Tyldesley refused to be tamed

and hit splendidly, the Australians began to concentrate their attack, not on the stumps, but wide of them. I have said that cricketers tried to finish their matches in three days, but on this occasion one side did not. To those who believe that negative bowling is a diabolical modern invention it must be said that it was practised in this game at least fifty years ago. Perhaps this was when it started. By the end of the second day England, despite their efforts, had scored only 169 for two wickets in three hours, which would be good going today in any Test match, but was not quick enough to give a winning lead.

In the morning the off-the-wicket bowling continued and while the England batsmen ' chased ' it, the crowd barracked lustily. Armstrong was bowling practically at the square-leg umpire, Uncle Walter said, while McLeod at the other end discharged the ball more or less in the direction of point. As did 20,000 Cornishmen of an earlier era, an even larger number of angry Leeds ' loiners ' wanted to know the reason why. Sarcastic. That's what Uncle Walter said they were. At all events scoring was so slow that England had to amass another 126 before Jackson felt he could safely close his innings, for declaration was always a risky procedure when you had Trumper against you. Then England took the field but, although the bowlers made a superlative effort, and the fall of some early wickets raised hopes, Noble, the Australian all-rounder, made a superlative effort, too. Australia could never have won, but they were determined not to lose and when the third day ended they had batted themselves into the position of an honourable draw.

The series of 1909 was a sad one for England, for the visiting Australians were not unconquerably strong and the home side were by no means deplorably weak. Yet Australia managed to concentrate their resources sufficiently to win two of the three completed games. They also had a little better of one of the two draws. It need hardly be said that England lost at Leeds. The first innings totals were almost exactly equal but England, after being set a mere 214 to win, failed wretchedly and were dismissed for 87. The old-fashioned word ' skittled ' is not too strong, for that is precisely what Cotter did to the English batsmen. The men he skittled were C. B. Fry, Hobbs, Sharp and Hirst and there was not a snick

or a mishit among all these dismissals. The stumps were hit
every time. In the first innings England had had an almost
equally tough, if not equally rough, time at the hands of
Macartney, who with his tantalising donkey-drops took seven
for 58. A dozen years later this slow bowler was to become
Australia's fastest batsman, another reminder of the high
value of the all-rounder. But in this game England's greatest
misfortune lay not in the virtual double failure of their batsman but in the accident to Jessop, who, after fielding for
an hour on the first day, ricked his back and, without even
having an innings, was seen no more on the cricket field that
summer. Fate had struck again . . .

This match, though bristling with bad luck, did not bristle
nearly as sharply as the corresponding game in 1921. An
England player told me afterwards : ' Everything happened
but an earthquake.' After the first day's play Jack Hobbs,
who had only just recovered from leg trouble, was operated
on for appendicitis, not actually at the wicket but, having
regard to the suddenness of the attack, very nearly so. (It is
a joyful and beautiful thought that, thirty-five years later,
Sir Jack is in far better health than he was then.) England
went in to face a total of over 400, out of which Macartney
had made 115, the only century hit by an Australian in that
series of Tests. The critics said that his pace was slow *for him*.
This was true, but even so, his pace, by modern Test match
standards, was moderately terrific. Lionel Tennyson, England's
captain, while fielding a bullet-like cover-drive from Macartney, split his hand, and twice batted gallantly with the other;
George Brown, also crippled, kept wicket and batted with fine
fortitude and a runner; Ducat was caught in the slips off a
ball that split his bat in two; and Douglas who, with Tennyson and Brown, had been the hero of the first innings, could
not field on the third day. This was because of the serious
illness of his wife, who had been struck down with appendicitis. In the end England lost by 219 runs and four casual-
ties. But wait.

The next Australian visit was in 1926, the year of the
General Strike, and there were other dramas besides. Before
the end of the first over of the Leeds Test two extraordinary
things had happened. Off the first ball sent down Sutcliffe
caught Bardsley and off the fifth Arthur Carr, one of Eng-

land's unlucky captains, who had put the Australians in on a pitch on which they were eventually to make 454, missed Macartney. This was an almost mortal error, for Macartney, in a batting display that would have made Blackpool's illuminations look subfusc, spread devastation among the England bowlers. We have already noted what he said : ' I felt like it and I went for everything.' He went for everything to such purpose that, out of the 235 put on for the second wicket (which should have fallen at 2) he scored 151, two thirds of them before lunch.

In Australia's total there were two other centuries and England's bowling was mown down like grass. Their batting also wilted before the wily Grimmett and the resistance movement did not seriously begin until it was taken up by the two Georges, Macaulay of Yorkshire and Geary of Leicestershire. The fiery stubbornness of the former blended boldly with the steadfastness of the latter in a stand which, while it did not quite save the follow-on, kept England's head above water long enough to turn defeat into a highly creditable draw.

II

And now, as the old novelists would say, we approach the incredible. The incredible is Bradman, who for nearly twenty years bestrode our petty world like a Colossus. The records show that he broke records everywhere, but he must have had an especial affection for Leeds. Looking back from 1948 to 1930, when his onslaughts began, he might well have been regarded as Leeds's most eminent citizen of the period, with a statue in City Square beside the Black Prince, and mounted not on a handsome bronze charger, but on a chain-gang of English bowlers, *couchant*. Sir Donald's knighthood was richly deserved on any grounds; it would have been well merited on one ground alone : Headingley, services to entertainment, at.

In 1930, on the first of his Test appearances at Headingley, he scored 334 in 375 minutes. That was Bradman's way. Where most batsmen would be happy with one hundred and elated with two, Bradman could seldom be prevailed on to settle for less than three. The Yorkshire crowd applauded wholeheartedly. This method of not merely defeating but overwhelming the opposition was one of which they approved in theory, though when inflicted on their own side, they may have regarded it a little wryly. This score of 334, though his first at Leeds, was his fourth successive century in Tests. The others had risen in a flamboyant curve from 123 to 131 and from 131 to 254. The holocaust of Headingley had begun.

In 1934 the massacre continued. On the first day of the Leeds Test England made 200. This, heaven knows, was a feeble score, but by six-thirty they appeared to have re-dressed the balance for Bowes had taken three quick wickets with only 37 on the board. The morning and the evening were the next day and only one wicket fell. It was not Bradman's. By the end of the innings he had made 304, hitting two sixes and forty-three fours. You could describe this second three-hundred at Leeds by many adjectives beginning with an m: magnificent, monumental, monolithic; for the spectator who hoped for one little flaw in infallibility, monotonous; and for the bowler whose figures were round about none for 150, monstrous. In spite of Australia's 584 the game was drawn, and England owed their escape to a cloud-burst and Maurice Leyland, in about equal proportions.

The summer of 1938 was a high-scoring season in which England also seemed to have learned the trick of piling up the score. This, you remember, was Hutton's year, in which a slender young Yorkshireman at the Oval beat Bradman's Test record and everyone else's with that historic 364. But it did not win England the rubber. At Leeds, a month before, Australia had won by five wickets, but it was, curiously enough, a low-scoring game which England might conceivably have won if (a) they had been able to bat *at all* after No. 6 and (b) if two catches had not been dropped in the last vital hour. Bradman did not rise to the 300 mark in this game. In fact, all he made was 103, but this in an innings in which five people failed to make double figures and six made only 35 between them. In the whole of the match only two players, one on each side, made 50 runs and one of the finest innings of the match was B. A. Barnett's 15 not out at the game's most palpitating point. The Leeds spectators knew great batting when they saw it and they knew that Bradman's innings of 103 was probably greater than his earlier gigantic totals of 334 and 304.

Even if 1938 saw a regression in quantity, if not in quality, Bradman came back with a vengeance in his next series, which was delayed until 1948, after the war. Australia trampled on England in their first post-war tour, repeating history as it had happened in 1921, and England's turn for triumph was not to come for another five years. The Australians had built up their cricket sooner and built it up well.

At Leeds in 1948 was played that fantastic game in which 1,723 runs were scored and Australia won by seven wickets fifteen minutes from time after England had declared. On the last day of this game, I was in my London office and listened to snatches of commentary as it came. A colleague of mine, a dour patriot, could scarcely control his emotion. He strode up and down and adjured the portable radio : ' But they can't get 'em; they can't *let* them get 'em.' But nobody could stop them getting 'em. Australia made 404 for three in 345 minutes and Bradman's share was 173 not out.

As he left the crease after this, his last great innings at Headingley, the crowd rose to him, cheering and clapping until throats and palms were sore. The crush was terrific and, as he set out upon his return to the pavilion, a posse of police had to force a way for him through the mob of enthusiastic admirers. Despite legal assistance, the pressure was so violent that for the moment movement was impossible and Bradman found himself standing opposite an old Yorkshireman whose wrinkled features were a study of conflicting emotions. It did not need a psychiatrist to interpret the old man's feelings : here was the greatest batsman in the world who had just swept his side to glorious triumph when, by all the laws of probability, they had no chance whatever. Here was the hated enemy, the man who had battered England's bowlers to a pulp; here was the foe of iron will, the ruthless tyrant who four times had brought England to the proud foot of a conqueror. Bradman was wonderful, Bradman was terrible. He admired him, he loved him, he hated him . . . Tears rained down the old man's cheeks. He stretched out his hand, but he could not speak. ' Ee,' he murmured. His lips moved, but no words came. And then there came forth the word which, without offence, by-passes the mere superlative, to denote the supreme, the infinite, the absolute, ' E,' he exclaimed, ' yer . . . booger !'

CHAPTER 14

THREE GOOD BOYS AND ONE OTHER

I

IF YOU were to ask me to name someone to stand as a typical professional cricketer of the best sort today, I should reply without hesitation: Willie Watson. Here is someone who, all his playing life, has shown the qualities that are attractive to the eye but are founded on something far deeper than attractiveness: a trim, 'wristy' style in both batting and fielding, good manners, good temper and a kind of clear integrity both as a cricketer and a man.

Every Yorkshire baby is said to be born with the spinning finger of his pretty little left hand clasped round the seam of a cricket ball. Watson's first toy was a football rather than a cricket ball. His father, who kept the Commercial Hotel at Paddock in Huddersfield, was also a professional footballer, and a very good one, and Willie and his brother grew up as 'natural' games players. Willie was a sound, though somewhat diffident player at school—he made his first century at the age of nine—and he was captain at both cricket and soccer of first the Huddersfield schoolboys' and then the Yorkshire schoolboys' elevens. When he won a scholarship to the local Grammar School, his athletic career was a tale of uninterrupted success. At fourteen he was going in first for Paddock in the Huddersfield League, the club that nurtured the famous Percy Holmes and another character just as remarkable in his way: Herbert Robinson, the mercurially enthusiastic president of the Huddersfield League. He is the sort of man whose hunches become a kind of inspired faith and his faith in Watson caused him to preach his protégé's merits day and night, in season and out of season. If Willie Watson's confidence in Willie Watson had been as great as Herbert Robinson's, he would have been a Bradman, at least. Robinson's only complaint was that his footwork was a tiny bit slow and when he mentioned this to George Hirst, the Grand Old Man said : ' Tell the lad to learn dancing.' Robinson thought this strange advice, but, strange as it seemed, it was highly successful.

When he left school he began an apprenticeship with a coachbuilding firm, but Huddersfield Town soon secured his full services and his career as a professional footballer was assured. The next summer a trial at the Headingley nets brought him a trial with the Yorkshire second eleven and his first two games brought him three successive ducks and a sense of failure. But in his next game he scored an attractive 63, which led to a trial with the first eleven and to another duck.

Then came the war, and Willie Watson joined the Army at the age of eighteen. While performing his duties as a physical instructor, he played a little cricket and a lot of football, appearing for the Army and for a Football Association eleven. It was in the last summer of the war that he played cricket for the local side—he was stationed in North Wales—against a touring Yorkshire eleven. He hit a century, added Brian Sellers to his admirers, and gained himself a game with Yorkshire in 1946 as soon as he was demobilised. At the same time he was given what was a remarkable opportunity in the circumstances, a Test trial in which he scored 61. It is interesting to glance at the names of those who played in that trial and see how far some of them have travelled.

There followed a quiet period in Watson's cricket career : he was doing nothing spectacular but holding his place as a valuable county member. In 1951 he played in all the Tests against South Africa, giving a badly needed stiffening to the English batting. Dudley Nourse's book on the tour speaks of him in admiring terms. In the meantime he had been playing First League Soccer for Sunderland, a team usually to be found near the top of the table, and he began to earn golden opinions as an unobtrusive but extremely effective left half. His skill in this position brought him four England caps and a visit to South America in a World Cup game, the result of which was disappointing. That England was heavily beaten was certainly not Watson's fault.

In the summer of 1952 he played once against the tourists from India and was in the first half-dozen in the season's batting averages. In 1953 he played his first Test against

Australia. It was the game at Lord's and it changed fortunes half a dozen times. On the evening of the penultimate day England went in to start the uphill task of making 343. Within a few minutes Hutton, Kenyon and Graveney were out for 12. So low were England's hopes of saving the game adjudged to be that no more than half the normal-sized crowd turned up the next morning.

First with Compton and then with Bailey, Watson stayed there. I saw every ball bowled that day and sincerely believe that Watson's innings should count among the truly great ones. This was indeed his finest hour. It was a triumph of character and concentration and when he was out at 109 England had saved the game. If Watson had been out early that morning it is hardly conceivable that England should have regained the Ashes.

He gave up a season's football in order to visit the West Indies with Hutton's 1953-54 team which, after a shaky start, courageously recovered and drew the rubber. In this series Watson was promoted to England's No. 2 position, a post which for some years has been difficult to fill. In the first Test he made an attractive hundred, but after one or two comparative failures, another No. 2 was chosen. My own view, respectfully tendered, is that Watson might have been persevered with, for a satisfactory No. 2 has still to be found. A further view is that Watson should have gone to Australia in 1954-55. Admittedly England won this series through certain excellencies, but, to put it mildly, there were gaps and one of them might have been filled by a stylish left-hand batsman who has never let England down. It would have been pleasant to think that, at the time, England's admirable captain had one burden the less on his shoulders.

If 1954 was a moderate year for Watson, as it was for most batsmen, 1955 was a splendid one. Just as his innings against the Australians at Lord's in 1953 was his finest individual performance, so 1955 was his finest season. If the figures are reckoned on a reasonable number of innings, he came second in the country's batting averages to so prolific a scorer as Peter May, and even this fact does not tell the whole story or show his full value to his side. There was a score of 174 not out which was far more than all the rest of the side managed to put together, and he pulled round the

Roses match for Yorkshire after an incredibly evil start. And there was his 214 not out, also after his county's bad start, against Worcestershire's by no means negligible bowling. But some comparatively small scores—a fifty or even a thirty against a rampant Surrey attack—were miracles of coolness and valour compared with which centuries on easy wickets against amiable bowling are as nought.

So here you have him : stylish and elegant at the wicket and swift and alert with a half-back's economy of movement in the field; and off the field, unassuming—far too unassuming, his friends say—courteous, friendly and, in the old-fashioned phrase, a gentleman in word and deed.

II

There have been greater players than George Cox, lately retired from the Sussex eleven, but there has never been a more joyous cricketer or a grander fellow. If you have seen him bat on one of his great days, you will instinctively have asked : why has this man not played for England? I have often asked this, particularly when he was making his practically inevitable centuries against Yorkshire, and the only answer seems to be that where some people have a dear little cherub who sits up aloft, Cox has often had a little black devil of ill-luck. He has also had the reputation of being a shaky starter. (You should have seen Bradman start sometimes . . .) When in form, he was just about the most attractive county batsman of his quite lengthy period : graceful, quick-scoring, prodigal of strokes, particularly those that fly along the ground through a tight off-side field. At cover he was as good as Robins, the best cover of the thirties; that is, Cox was practically the only man in England who could have stopped his own cover drives.

I call George Cox a 'good boy,' not because he would claim to be more virtuous than his fellow-citizens, but because he has always been a good cricketer, a good son, a good coach and a good companion. From 1931 till 1949 he was George Cox Junior, because his father, George R. Cox, was one of the old Sussex stalwarts, from the days when Fry and Ranji made the county a prodigious batting side but a heavy burden lay on a limited number of bowlers, one of whom was 'old

George,' slow left-hand and an indefatigable worker. His most famous feats were slightly fantastic: seven for 8 against Derbyshire in 1920, five for 0 against Somerset in 1921, and seventeen for 126 against Warwickshire in 1926 at the age of fifty-two. At forty-seven he had a season when he took 81 wickets and hit 844 runs. If you were going to be a cricketer, that was the sort of father to choose.

Not only was young George Cox a vividly attractive batsman to watch: he saved his more scintillating displays for the scourging of the stronger counties, notably Yorkshire. In his last ten playing years his average against Yorkshire was about 100. His personality has the same effervescent quality as his batting. I remember reproving him for making 142 against Yorkshire in the last county match of the 1938 season, hitting 100 out of 114 in an hour. It was an exhibition of pure pyrotechnics. ' Ah,' said George without perfunctory modesty, ' I took 198 off them the year after that. And,' he added cheerfully, ' we lost.'

In a sense that summer of 1938 was a typical George Cox season; he had done splendidly the year before, but after a century in the second match he suffered a patch so long and sticky that he found himself in the second eleven; but, fighting back, he finished the year with a positive star shower of 405 in six innings. In 1947 he had an even vivider individual outburst—it was practically a volcanic eruption—in which he hit 569 in five following innings. That was Cox's way. Between the end of the war and his retirement there was only one season in which he did not make his thousand runs. In 1946 he had a glorious innings of 234—you might have called it an escapade—against the Indian tourists; 1948 was his poor year when he made a little under 900 runs, but he came back in 1949 when, just for old friendship's sake, he hammered Yorkshire bowling to the tune of 212 not out. (At Leeds, mark you.) In 1950, which was his wonderful year, he delighted spectators with half a dozen hundreds and ended the season with an average of 50.

In 1951 he took a richly deserved benefit and it is typical of the erratic way in which fortune treats him that the weather was horrid. Why fortune could not be friendlier to such a friendly chap I cannot think. It is also characteristic that when Sussex batted on a dire wicket, George Cox made top score,

defending valiantly with a fifty that must have been as valuable to Sussex as almost any of his fifty centuries. In 1953
he made another of his almost monotonous hundreds against
Yorkshire and right to the end of his last season he played
his own delightful game.

There can hardly have been a man so well-liked by his
fellow professionals both in his own county and in all the
others. He has a twinkling solemn humour. I saw him play in
a 'friendly' game for Sussex against the Duke of Norfolk's
eleven on the beautful ground at Arundel Castle. As George
took guard, the announcer who was giving a commentary on
the game made a trifling mistake. ' And here,' he said, ' is Ken
Suttle . . .'

Instantly George whipped round, bent to Suttle's lower
height and played the ball with a typical left-handed Suttle
stroke. Not at all funny as described, but, visually, it had
several thousand spectators rolling in the green aisles.

George has one very serious joke : his hundred ducks. He
has not, in fact, made a hundred ducks, but he claims (quite
boastfully for a modest man) that he has come nearer to this
beautiful ideal than any other batsman. He said at the end
of the 1955 season that his score had reached the tantalising
total of 95, but the statisticians, as far as I know, have not
checked it. I almost feel inclined to say that a duck by George
Cox could be as delightful as a century by some less mercurial
batsman. He has stated that two ducks eluded him in 1955
because on the first occasion he hit a catch to the one fieldsman who would drop anything and, on the other, to the one
fieldsman who was so small that it flew over his head.

It is not every cricketer who has great personal charm;
there are more important, though no more attractive, qualities. Cox is one of the rare ones who has the sturdy qualities
and the charm as well. A famous critic once said of 'old
George' that he was a ' man of stubborn disposition and impeccable integrity.' The impeccable integrity has been be-
queathed to his son, plus a keen intelligence, plus likeability
to the highest degree. It is characterstic of George Cox that he
played his last few games for his county with a badly damaged
thumb. There were certain duties and pleasures he would not
miss. ' I want to finish in the middle,' he said, ' not in the
pavilion.'

For several winters he has travelled to South Africa to take up coaching appointments and I believe it impossible that he should fail as a first class coach, for, to a wide technical knowledge, he adds kindliness, optimism, an almost senti-mental desire to help and, what so many coaches lack, a genuine ability to instruct.

Like Watson, he has had an honourable winter career in association football, though he did not gain an international cap. When he retired from the Sussex eleven in September, 1955, he went off to Winchester to replace his old team-mate, Ted Bowley, as cricket, and soccer, coach. It is always a sad time for a first class cricketer when he leaves his old com-rades and the scenes of his battles, victories and embarrass-ments; it is a pleasant solace that he can fade from the scene to another, still green and still pleasant, where he can teach the young to emulate his own successes and avoid his errors. Cox, I prophesy, will be in the highest flight among coaches. The school whose motto is ' Manners Makyth Man ' could not have made a happier choice.

III

Because of my fanatical, perhaps foolish, searches for pos-sible successors to the great all-rounders of ' my time,' I was delighted with the success in 1955 of a young man who scored a thousand runs and just missed two hundred wickets. Some years ago at a dinner I sat next to a G.I.P. (genuinely inter-esting person) who, after a long career in the field and the committee room, spends his time looking out for new talent. ' I'm nursing three lads,' he said. ' One is a certainty to play for England; the second is a probable and the third is a possible.'

Now the odd thing is that of these three youngsters, No. 3 has had a chance and remains just a possible, the well-backed No. 1 has very slightly faltered, though he is still young enough to come sturdily back, and No. 2, the middle one, is Fred Titmus.

He started very young and is still only twenty-three; if he does not go a long way, many people will be disappointed and some judges far more knowledgeable than myself will have been wrong. He started modestly—it is even a modest

act to be born in Kentish Town—and though at his primary
and grammar schools he showed promising talent at both
cricket and football, he did not set the Thames on fire. His
first experiences in first class cricket were modest, too. He was
only eighteen when he first played for Middlesex. He played
again in 1952. Like the House of Peers, he did nothing in
particular, but did it at least so well that the following year
he gained an extended trial.

In this, his first full season, he showed the benefit of the
coaching he had received by taking 105 wickets and making
500 odd runs. The coaching came from J. W. (Young Jack)
Hearne, one of Middlesex's best all-rounders, whose every
action, whether in batting, bowling or fielding, was full of
grace. The Australians against whom he played in 1911-12
were among his greatest admirers. While Titmus has not
acquired Hearne's elegance he has learnt something of his
economy of movement. He bowled deceptively and he bowled
a better length than youngsters usually do. Here was a boy
who was worth persevering with. The following season he
made genuine progress: he took 111 wickets and 21 catches
and made 649 runs, including two obstinate knocks of 56 and
34 in one of those heart-stopping matches with Somerset which
Middlesex won by one wicket, during a last over when practically everybody else was too wrought up to bat, bowl or
even run anybody out.

The year 1955 has been Titmus's best so far. Everybody
knows his figures for the season and nobody can say that they
are not impressive. He played creditably in two Tests and
the standard of his fielding was certainly above the contemporary standard. He played a hero's part in the Players' narrow victory over the Gentlemen. This game was something of
a Leicestershire holiday, with centuries from Palmer on one
side and Tompkin on the other, but Titmus, in batting, bowling and fielding, showed himself a true all-rounder, cool and
reliable in times of crisis.

In county games his batting has become concentrated and
tenacious; his bowling remains apparently innocent, so innocent that he looks like a nice young curate putting up a few
easy donkey-drops with a soft ball to the little boys at the
Sunday School picnic. The little boys hit out. Sometimes they
give the ball quite a hard knock, but much oftener they miss

it and are bowled or caught off a stroke which went anywhere but where they meant it. And during 1955 as many as nearly two hundred boys got themselves out. They must have thought it extraordinary. On 29th August, 1955, he took his 155th wicket for Middlesex, thus beating Albert Trott's record for a Middlesex bowler in 1900. Extraordinary indeed.

And the future? Nobody knows. But the virtues of steadiness, persistence and a technical skill much higher than it looks from the boundary will, I think, go on reaping greater rewards. And even if they do not go as far as I think they will, there will still be a very nice lad.

IV

Sammy Woods was never called a good boy by anybody. He would not have understood the term. To begin with, he was an Australian and a fast bowler. He was also a Rugby footballer, rendered fierce by having learnt his football at a soccer school. He was about the fastest bowler who ever played for an English school, just as K. L. Hutchings was the hardest-hitting batsman. It was generous of Australia, one feels, to send one of her most flamboyant sons to take on the semblance of an Englishman, but at heart he was as typical an Australian as Emmott Robinson was a Yorkshireman.

At Cambridge, where he did everything except read for his degree, he was, on the cricket and rugger fields, not so much a shining light as a flaming jumping cracker. Before he went up, Oxford cricketers had been having things all their own way, but during the four years that Sammy was in the Cambridge eleven, he first got them down and then held them down. The first game was a draw, with Oxford saved by rain while having much the worst of it. Cambridge won the other three. In every instance the vital factor was the bowling of Woods, abetted by the semi-miraculous wicketkeeping of that other rugger genius, Gregor McGregor. When Woods was captain he saw that the young F. S. Jackson—of all people—was worrying as to whether his form was good enough to warrant a blue. 'Here,' said Sammy, 'stop worrying about the dam' thing. Here it is, anyway . . .'

That fourth Varsity match swept its way to a finish equal in intensity to Cobden's match of 1870. Cambridge were

set only 90 to win after making Oxford follow on, but the
pitch was bad, the light was worse and wickets kept falling
all the time. When eight wickets were down, the match had
become a tie. Sammy came down the steps amid the encircling gloom, minus blue cap, minus pads, minus gloves. If he
had been without trousers, which might possibly have happened, for he had had no idea that No. 10 would be called on
to bat, nobody would have noticed because of the almost
Stygian darkness. As it was, he had a strange bat, and hardly
saw the first ball as it came to him. Nevertheless he hit it hard
and true to the rails for four and Cambridge had won another
' mad ' match.

Sammy's Cambridge career was the most colourful of his
time and his fame at cricket and rugger were only equalled
by his skill in avoiding contamination from mere academic
learning. But Cambridge played the game with Sammy just
as he played the game by Cambridge and Nelson's blind-eye
telescope was matched by the kindly myopia which afflicted
the university authorities when confronted by Sammy's
chronic absence from lectures and allergy to examinations.
Their reward is in heaven.

I remember mentioning one or two details in the scholastic
career of S. M. J. Woods to an earnest young undergraduate
nephew of mine.

' You would never,' he pronounced severely, ' get away with
it now.'

' Maybe,' I said unoriginally, ' but don't you wish you
could.'

When Woods went down from Cambridge he joined
Somerset, that glorious county which has seldom been successful in normal day-to-day cricket but over the years has made
a habit of trouncing teams at the top of the table. It was
Sammy who helped them to rise from second to first class
status, and who liked to knock 70 or 80 off Lockwood and
Richardson when they were the best bowlers in the world.
Sammy was at his best as a swashbuckling swordsman in a
fighting team. He loved combat for its own sake. When you
are a hostile fast bowler, a lynx-eyed hard-hitting bat and a
suicide-prone fieldsman, no game is lost until the very last
wicket has fallen. And Sammy's fighting spirit pulled many
a game out of the fire.

He bowled at you with tremendous zest and it did his heart good to see your stumps crashing, but when you played him well, he bore you no malice. Sir Pelham Warner, while a schoolboy, played against him and hit a fast ball from him hard past extra cover for four. 'Well played, little fellow,' cried Sammy. But next ball the little fellow's bails flew different ways.

He was a genial giant; a big man in ordinary clothes who looked, when stripped, a great deal bigger. *The Jubilee Book of Cricket* says: 'The power in his huge thighs, long back and knotted shoulders is colossal.' In his great days he fairly catapulted the ball at the batsman, all his heart and soul were in the delivery. When he was older and had lost some of his fire, he would confess that he was only 'pretending to bowl,' and he would make up for his diminished pace by an expression of increased ferocity. 'Where will you have it?' he would demand of the man at the crease, just to cheer him up. 'On the 'eart or the 'ead?' But, of course, he did not want to batter you personally. It was your stumps he was after. He had a slow ball, too, which was a cruel deceiver. When you had braced yourself to withstand a series of thunderbolts, this slow one, delivered with the same intimidating action, had a paralysing effect. And when it bowled you all over the shop, Sammy would roar with gargantuan laughter.

A happy hunting ground for Sammy was the Gentlemen v. Players match. There was a long period, as we know, when the Gentlemen, under W.G.'s dominance, held absolute sway, but even the Old Man could not keep young for ever and it was in the early nineties that Sammy brought fresh life and vigour to the amateurs. W.G.'s batting had been paramount, as was Bradman's in a later era, but the Gentlemen had been weak in bowling. The advent of Sammy had the effect of a blood transfusion.

In his first match, at the Oval in 1888, he took five for 58 in a game in which the Players made only 176 but won by an innings and 39. It was three years later, also at the Oval, that Sammy produced almost exactly the opposite result by hearty, hostile fast bowling, including Ulyett, William Gunn, Abel, Barnes and Briggs among his victims. At Lord's in 1894 he performed, while bowling unchanged with F. S. Jackson, what has always been reckoned as one of the outstanding bowling feats of the long series. The figures were:

	First Innings				Second Innings			
	O	M	R	W	O	M	R	W
Woods	... 24.2	8	61	4	21.4	6	63	2
Jackson	... 24	8	36	5	24	7	41	7

He took five for 50 at Lord's in 1896 and six for 111 in 1898; in 1900 he was captain in what was probably the most astonishing Gentlemen v. Players match ever played. Left 161 behind on the first innings, the Players saw their opponents pile up 339, including a second century by the peerless R. E. Foster, and were set a nice round figure of 500 to win. The heroes of the assault that followed were Abel, who just missed his century; Hayward (111) and J. T. Brown (163), whose late-cutting was executed with what the chronicler calls 'merciless brilliance.' When Rhodes came in, 16 were still needed, but a situation like this was meat and drink to Rhodes. At six-thirty the scores were equal and Woods was entitled to take his men off the field, leaving the match a tie. Impulsively, however, he seized the ball and sent down a delivery off which Rhodes made the winning hit and the game was over.

As a county man Sammy gave his heart and soul to Somerset. He never failed to bowl with every ounce of his strength and every year he conscientiously tried to improve his batting. Sometimes, as at Brighton in 1895, he would attack the bowling murderously so that it reeled under the shock while Sammy piled up his second hundred. A couple of years later he did almost the same thing, and kept on doing it; he must have *liked* Sussex bowling. His batting all the time was brave and free.

I like to think of him on that bitter day in May, 1895, when W.G. was battling to score his hundredth century. It was so cold that from time to time a flurry of snowflakes played about the Old Man's beard. (Where's your Hermit's Derby now?) Grace batted with concentrated stubbornness and Sammy bowled with a fury that only Tom Richardson could have surpassed. The Old Man had reached 98, the scorer put up two figures; then, and not till then, Sammy gave him a nice one. The deed was done. Champagne followed.

In the oft-described game in which Somerset beat the Champions by 279 runs, it is recorded that Sammy never spoke until the Somerset players were safely in their hotel and then he uttered the one word: '*Magnum!*'

Feeling the wear and tear of his years a little, he somewhat sadly resigned the captaincy in 1906, but went on playing. As he was but a shadow of his former self, so was Somerset. Under the captaincy of Sammy's rugger-playing companion, John Daniell, Somerset recovered. But never has there been since anyone who could delight the cricket world with the fire, the fury and the fun of Sammy Woods.

CHAPTER 15

FESTIVALS OF BRITAIN

I

FESTIVAL cricket has become a phrase which suggests a truce to dull care and a welcome to frivolity, the general idea being that a cricketer is entitled to a bit of fun after the stern battles of the county championship, pretty much as the man in the ballad seeks his little grey home in the west when the toil of the long day is o'er. It is a pleasing thought and, unlike so many pleasing thoughts, it has an element of fact in it.

At Scarborough in the north and Hastings in the south festival time comes at the end of the season, when dull care can be cast aside without loss of prestige or much-needed points and when September sunshine may warm the heart of the stolidest stonewaller. There is also a festival of the west played on the delightful Torquay ground which has given a great deal of pleasure of late years. Yet the gayest (or to the most bigoted and persecuting northerner) at least the second gayest of all festivals is one which displays two often fiercely contested county matches on which the championship may precariously hang. True, the Canterbury Festival takes place at August Bank Holiday at the same time as a Roses match, three hundred miles away, hurls Yorkshire and Lancashire into one of their two annual death-grapples. Yet, however hard Kent may be fighting, cricket at Canterbury holds summer in its hand.

Variety, if not the spice of life, is at least a guarantee that the world is full of a number of things. Bramall Lane is one good thing and Canterbury quite another, for there the battle-murder-and-sudden-death aspect of the game is exchanged for that other side of cricket which is compounded of grace, skill and charm under a summer heaven. Here, on a great stretch of emerald turf lined with friendly trees and gaily-decked tents, the game goes on, as it has gone on for a hundred years, amid the live murmur of a summer day. The scene is so informal that one of the trees actually grows inside the playing area. Neville Cardus has said : ' An innings by Woolley at Canterbury is a pastoral . . .'

You could not have a vivider description : it does not mean that action is wanting but that action takes place against the eternal background of English country life. It is Barrie's authentic rural cricket match in buttercup time, seen and heard through the trees. There are some stands but they form less a part of the scene than the marquees and the bunting. The same sun shines down (sometimes disconcertingly) on the windscreens of a thousand cars that once glittered on the coachwork and harness of a thousand horse-drawn carriages, dog-carts and brakes.

Every year since the beginning of the Festival, the day's cricket has been crowned by a performance in which amateur actors, to their great delight, appear on the stage with professional actresses. In 1842 the play performed was *The Poor Gentleman* by Coleman, with a prologue and an epilogue written and spoken by Tom Taylor, friend of Thackeray, editor of *Punch* and himself a fine cricketer. Nine years later the players first used the name, Old Stagers, which has graced their theatre bills ever since and now, each year, the play is followed by an epilogue which has transformed the original monologue into a topical revue culminating with the entry of the Spirits of Kent, the I. Zingari and the Old Stagers in person.

The cricket that the St. Lawrence ground has seen forms an endless pageantry of green and gold. The names of the great Kent cricketers are magic names, and they stretch from the days of Fuller Pilch and the ' kind and manly Alfred Mynn,' through Lord Harris who moulded Kent as Lord Hawke moulded Yorkshire, to the Kent elevens of the golden age, gleaming with the names of K. L. Hutchings, Colin Blythe and Frank Woolley. The last of these played almost throughout the whole length of the inter-war period, alongside players like B. H. Valentine and Leslie Ames, who is one of the most modest as he is one of the most remarkable of cricketers. The Kentish heroes since the second war have been Godfrey Evans, worthy to be named with any wicket-

keeper of the golden age, and Douglas Wright, who can do
more tricks with a fastish ball than most bowlers can do with
a slow one. And it may be that Colin Cowdrey has before
him a career more glittering than any of the others. The long
picaresque drama never lacks leading characters . . .

The Canterbury Festival was at times almost a family
festival. E. M. Grace in 1861 took all ten wickets in one
innings and made 192 not out; Fred made a decent score
when he was only fifteen; and W.G. himself ran riot on
many occasions. In 1868 he made two centuries in the match,
South of the Thames v. North of the Thames, the second
being 102 not out during an innings in which only two other
persons made double figures. The following year he made
another century for M.C.C. against Kent and in 1871, one
of his earlier great years, he made 117 in the same game. In
1874 he played in a match between a mixed eleven of Kent
and Gloucestershire against the rest of England and complained of 'fairly hard luck' because, while he made 121
runs in the second innings, he got only 94 in the first. In the
second match of that year's Festival, he took another century
for the M.C.C. off Kentish bowling, scoring 123 out of 174
in just over a couple of hours.

It was in 1876, another of his 'great' years, that he compiled the mightiest score of his mighty first class career. In
that season only one of his seven centuries was made at Canterbury. The circumstances were fantastic, when you consider
that M.C.C. had gone in, and were obliged to follow on,
against a big score by Kent to which Lord Harris, batting at
the top of his form, had contributed 154. This was the first
time the batsmen's names were printed on the telegraph board
and the attendant got the laugh of the century by mislaying
the 'H' and putting the Kent captain up as ARRIS. Altogether 1,174 runs were scored for the loss of thirty-one
wickets, and of this total W.G., going in first when M.C.C.
followed on, made the almost incredible total of 344 in an
innings of 557. He has confessed that as there was no hope
of saving the match and he wanted to catch a train to Bristol
as soon as possible, he opened his shoulders and hit out at
everything. What is even more remarkable is that he had only
one partner who made anything approaching a decent score
and that none of the rest—they were playing twelve a side—

made more than fifteen. 'I nearly succeeded in playing out time,' was his modest comment, 'being eventually caught for 344'—Oh, hard luck, sir!—'with the score at 546.'

After battles long ago on such a gargantuan scale, the Festival in this prosaic century seems a little less exciting. Yet it has had its moments. In the early nineteen-hundreds Kent's chief Festival opponents were Lancashire, Sussex and Surrey. There were many draws, owing either to heavy scoring or heavier rain. Kent won three victories of similar pattern over Surrey when the bowling of W. M. Bradley (very fast) and of Blythe (cruelly deceptive) prevailed over the almost solitary batting resistance of Tom Hayward, who performed wonders of defence while the rest of his side perished.

Later Hampshire became popular Festival opponents, and in 1908 they snatched victory from Kent by one wicket in a thrilling game, when Newman and Stone, the old Hants wicketkeeper, hung on, with a single here and a single there, till the very end. If they had not, Kent would have won by at least 50 runs.

In 1926, Canterbury was given a game for the gods. Hants at the first attempt were demolished for a derisory score by Freeman who took five for 43 and Kent, with swift centuries by Hardinge and Chapman (England's winning captain against Australia that year) piled up a towering score. Easy victory seemed assured. Then Hants came back. I have never seriously believed that truth is stranger than fiction. I know too much about fiction. But once in a way you get in real life a game more romantic than any fiction editor would dare to print. The incredible Philip Mead (still alive and may heaven bless him) scored 175 not out and, in the company of an unknown amateur named J. P. Parker, put on 270 in 170 minutes for the eighth wicket. Kent were left with a severely limited time in which to get the runs but, just to show that in a match like that the picturesque possibilities cannot be exhaused, Woolley and Chapman started off with a terrific burst of hitting and just beat the clock. My own feeling is of wonderment as to what happened to J. P. Parker and whether he ever played such a heroic innings again.

There was another exciting finish in 1953 in which Hants made it a draw, but only just. My own most treasured recollection of post-war Canterbury was of watching Tony Pawson

M

for the first time—an England player, I thought, if ever I saw one—running between the wickets like a Pegasus outside-right and scoring 90 while his partners puffed and panted. That he did not play for England has always been a source of regret to me.

Canterbury is indeed a cornerstone of English cricket. The flags wave, the great green expanse remains the same corner of an English field that it always has been and the ancient tree at third man (or long-on if you happened to be batting at the other end) still stands. Like the meteor flag of England, it has braved the battle and the breeze; and, like a certain eye geographically placed to the north of Katmandhu, it for ever gazes down.

II

Hastings is a name connected with a date, perhaps the only date in English history which has enjoyed adequate publicity. Another date important to Hastings is 1887, Queen Victoria's jubilee year, which saw the first beginnings of the September Festival. The insignia of festival are much the same everywhere : flags in primary colours, bunting which flirts in the breeze, and a certain amount of improvised seating in the form of striped deck-chairs, but of the three major Festival grounds, only Hastings has a theatrical backdrop of a geniune medieval castle.

In the early days the matches arranged were chosen according to the availabilities of the end of the season. Sometimes it was a North v. South or a Gentlemen v. Players or a Gentlemen of the South v. Gentlemen of the North. Even if later some of the 'bigger' names tended to steal away to Scarborough, the games were always cheerful, colourful and gay. The first Gentlemen v. Players game (in 1889) found a hero in Mr. H. Pigg, who sounds as though he ought to have come straight out of Jorrocks. This practically anonymous amateur passed summary sentence on a Players eleven which was strong enough to contain William Gunn, Abel, Albert Ward, Peel, Ulyett, Attewell and Lohmann. In the second innings he took seven for 55 and was in himself the main reason why (a) the Gentlemen snatched a victory by one wicket and (b) a crowd, led by his worship the mayor, subsequently surged in front of the pavilion, 'cheering itself hoarse.' Not only did the demon Pigg shatter the Players' wickets. In the first innings he made top score with the bat, 35, being only surpassed by Mr. Extras, who beat him by one.

There was a Gentleman v. Players match in 1892 in which the great Sammy Woods took eight wickets for 46 in a first innings onslaught, but when the Players followed on, Abel made a flawless century and almost everybody else made 50. Sammy was very nearly in the position of being obliged to bowl at both ends. Even a slow jog-trot bowler might have flinched from the ordeal, but Sammy, bowling at his own furious pace, actually sent down sixty-five overs.

The mighty W.G. allowed few grounds to pass without the tribute of a century and, though he invaded Hastings fairly late in life, he came as another William, another conqueror. In 1894, when he was forty-six, he came down to lend distinction to a South v. North match and made his only Hastings century. He showed some reluctance in turning out at all, for, as he said, 'the match was played very late in the year, and I had to leave some capital partridge shooting.' He cheered up however, sufficiently to score 131 and to chuckle over the fact that a ball from Mold cannoned off his pad on to his wicket without dislodging the bails. It must have been the first and last time this ever happened to Mold, a born dislodger, if ever there was one.

Since the second world war there have been some variations in picking sides: South of England v. Sir Pelham Warner's Eleven, Under Thirty-Two v. Over Thirty-Two, an England XI v. a Commonwealth side. In 1955 there were moments of splendour when the most festival-minded of contemporary batsmen, Roy McLean, galvanised a moribund game into life by flogging England's best bowlers in all directions. No other opponent, certainly no Australian or other South African, has consistently hit Tyson back over Tyson's head. That was a battle of Hastings worth watching . . .

III

When I was a lad, my family took me to the sea every year. The sea was a thing they kept at Scarborough; indeed, it was quite a long time before I realised that other places

might have a sea, too. Even today, half a century later, I
have a lingering feeling that, compared with the sea at Scarborough, all other seas were vastly inferior. 'For where'er,'
sang Nanki-Poo,

> 'For where'er our country's banner may be planted,
> All other local banners are defied.'

For me the sea at Scarborough was a kind of aqueous
Union Jack. The sea was the main feature, but there was a
full supporting programme. There was hokey-pokey, a sweet-
meat far more luscious than the mere ice-cream you got at
home, sold to you by a swarthy, piratical-looking character of
the Latin race from a gaudy gilded palace on wheels. There
were the donkeys, those high-spirited creatures, if you wanted
to ride like cowboys and Indians, and little goat-carriages, if
you were minded to ride in a miniature Cinderella's coach.
But the most dazzling equipage—and I never saw it anywhere
else but at Scarborough—was the open carriage where the
cabby sat, not on the box, for there was no box, but astride
the horse. In fact, he was not a cabby at all; he was a jockey,
with racing colours as gay as a rainbow. To ride in that carriage gave you the same sensation as a modern small boy
might feel if he were lolling back in a jeep, with Lester
Piggott sitting well forward on the bonnet.

I remember the bathing, too, though, for myself, I merely
paddled. Bathing was still on the secret list and was virtually
carried on behind an iron curtain, from prefabricated houses
on wheels. These were drawn down to the sea by large cart-
horses, patient semi-aquatic creatures, that looked, as they
entered the North Sea, like gentle hippopotami. From what
was now the front door of the machine, a shivering shame-
faced figure emerged, clad in a costume like a badly inflated
balloon. The upper half was indescribable and lower half
unmentionable. The male bathers were incarcerated—held in
protective custody—in another block of prefabs half a mile
along the shore, for, of course, there was no co-educational
bathing then. Altogether it was a slightly grim business.

I did not know about cricket until I was practically grown
up—ten or eleven, at least. I did not then know the story of
the Festival and its historic Nine Days; all I knew was that
my Uncle Walter took me to the North Marine Road ground
to see the Australians. This was the year when F. S. Jackson

captained England, won the toss in all five Test matches, headed his country's batting and bowling averages, and retained the Ashes in a confident grip. England recently won back and then held on to the Ashes under the captaincy of a very great batsman and a very bad tosser, and my almost fanatical admiration for Hutton was modified by the wishful feeling that, if only he had learnt Jackson's secret recipe for spinning the coin, the Ashes might have stayed in England indefinitely. Peter May, his legitimate heir, is compounded of all the manly and cricketing virtues, but he, too, has shown occasional flaws in his tossing technique. It is matter that requires serious attention.

So deeply had the Australian morale been dented by Jackson's triumphant (and clairvoyant) tossing, that at Scarborough the Australian captain, Joe Darling, stripped himself like an all-in wrestler for one last effort. But it was in vain. Jackson won the toss and England batted. I have said, England, but, of course the team was not called England, but C. I. Thornton's Eleven. Yet, apart from its stumper, old David Hunter, who ought to have been an England man, anyhow, the eleven was virtually an England eleven, starting with MacLaren, Spooner and Tyldesley, Lancashire's pride, and having Hirst, Rhodes and Haigh, my own particular heroes, near the other end. It was Jackson, however, who dominated the day, and if there has ever been a better century than his 123 that day, I should like to have seen it. He was not an elegant artist, like Spooner; he played the ordinary, orthodox strokes, but he hit the ball so hard that it looked as if it was badly frightened as it skittered over the boundary-line. As it happened, David Hunter, the last man in, made 17 not out, while those indisputably great men, Hirst, Rhodes, Denton and Haigh, hardly made 17 between them. I had seen the Hon. F. S. Jackson make a century in his triumphant year and even Scarborough's hokey-pokey could hardly taste sweeter than the thought of it . . .

Of course, the world and the Festival were not new, just because I was young. The Festival had been going even then for at least thirty years and was already a cherished institution. The world had existed even longer.

There are certain names—almost sacred names—which have successively become connected with this September

M*

ritual. Mr. C. I. Thornton's Eleven. Mr. H. D. G. Leveson-Gower's Eleven. Mr. T. N. Pearce's Eleven . . . That is the way the tradition has been carried on. In so far as it can be said that anybody invented Scarborough Festival, it was C. I. (' Buns ') Thornton who, in intervals of hitting sixes, agreed, back in the seventies, to arrange a match between the local team (which happened in effect to be practically a Yorkshire side) and the visitors, who included several of the famous Walker brothers of Southgate and, of course, C. I. Thornton himself.

Thornton was as mighty a hitter as Nimrod was a hunter. There was something about Scarborough—perhaps it was the seaside air—which lent power to his mighty arm. It was, I think, James Shaw who used to wake up in the middle of the night in a cold sweat, wondering what would happen if ' Mr. Thornton was to hit one slap back at me.'

Thornton was quite unconscionable in the way his hitting would break windows in the houses round the ground. Once he broke the same window twice with successive balls, and when the house-owner not unreasonably protested, he said thoughtfully : ' Well, perhaps you ought to leave it open . . . '

The Festival has had a happy history. The matches in the early days were M.C.C. (C. I. Thornton's Eleven) v. Yorkshire, Gentlemen v. Players, or I. Zingari v. Gentlemen of England. An interesting and popular alternative fixture which grew up was that between C. I. Thornton's Eleven and the team that was going abroad to Australia or South Africa the following autumn. Right from the earliest Festivals, in those golden days of late summer, something fascinating was always going on.

In 1878, when the present ground was called the ' new ' ground, C. I. Thornton had one of his more merciful matches and hit the ball out of sight only four times. It was eight years later that he hit eight sixes, including the famous onslaught on Scarborough's Trafalgar Square. (' He never told me,' said his wife, ' whether he was playing at Lord's or the Oval.') It was in 1881 that the young man who was to become the great Lord Hawke played for his county for the first time and played extremely well.

The field is indeed full of shades . . . There is something

most unghostlike about the burly bearded figure of . . . who else could it be? In the first Scarborough Gentleman v. Players match, W. G. Grace made 174 out of 247 and the Gentlemen, as they often did in Grace's time, won by an innings. In 1894 came Ranji for the first time and two years later came Jessop, a more exciting pyrotechnician even than C. I. Thornton. How beautiful they were, the lordly ones . . .

And there were the great warriors of Yorkshire's golden era, released from the rigours of the county championship (which they had no doubt carried off in triumph), enjoying their ease in the gayer air of the Festival and just *playing* at cricket . . . Brown, Tunnicliffe, Denton and, of course, the epic figures of Hirst and Rhodes. In 1901 there was an Over 30 v. Under 30 match in which Hirst, who was only a week under thirty, hit twenty-seven fours in an innings of 163. And then, hating to do things by halves, he took five wickets for 40. Over a long period of years, he was an institution at Scarborough, as he was elsewhere, as player, then as umpire, and then a revered figure as a spectator. We ne'er shall look upon his like again.

In 1913 Scarborough saw its last Gentlemen v. Players game before the first war. Sir Pelham Warner says it was in a sense ' the perfect cricket match' because all four innings were nearly equal. Some glorious performers were on view. Although Jessop made 117 (two sixes and seventeen fours), sturdy batting by Hirst and Relf, plus a slight Jessopian impersonation by Bill Hitch, took the players just four runs ahead. The Gentlemen's second innings was lit by a radiant century from Aubrey Faulkner and the Players, set 252 to win, collapsed ignominiously. Six wickets went down for 63 and even when Hirst and Booth added 80 by a stubborn rearguard action, eight wickets had fallen and 106 were still needed. Booth remained steadfast, while breathless spectators watched another glorious knock—and knock is the right word —by Hitch, but when the Yorkshireman was out, Douglas clean bowled Dolphin and the Gentlemen had won by six runs. Gentlemen and Players did not appear at Scarborough again until 1919. M. W. Booth, that splendid young all-rounder, never came back.

The glamour of Scarborough is not imprisoned in any past golden age. Consult your last few *Wisdens* and you will see that Scarborough has regularly been a scene of riot and prodigality. In 1952 the Yorkshire v. M.C.C. match saw Hutton and Peter May hit two centuries each and who shall say which was the most glorious of the four? If 1952 was a riot, 1953 was an orgy. In the M.C.C. match Hutton and Lowson made centuries; in the Gentlemen v. Players there were four hundreds, including a double one from Hutton the Master; and in the Australian visitors' farewell game, which the parting guests won by two wickets, Richie Benaud, who had not had a particularly good tour, went berserk and hit eleven sixes in an innings which, for sheer fireworks, out-Jessoped Jessop.

In 1955 there was a technicoloured finish to the match between T. N. Pearce's Eleven and the visiting South Africans. Though the game began soberly, brilliance would keep breaking in. There was a rapid-fire century from Endean, followed by colossal hitting by Winslow and Cheetham, who hit sixes to corners of the map of Scarborough that even C. I. Thornton had never thought of. Graveney made 159 by methods that were dazzling even for Graveney, and, in the final reply, South Africa raced to victory over the clock at the rate of 100 an hour while Cheetham, happy skipper of a happy side, made the winning hit off the fifth ball of the last over. Sometimes even the story book comes into its own.

Scarborough cricket, with its flags flying and its bands playing, is cricket's high festival. To vary the metaphor, it is the champagne of the game, the best wine kept till the last. Life is real, life is earnest and the county championship is, most of the time, its goal. But as the autumn sunshine lingers it is possible to think wistfully of David Denton who, as you remember, 'played at Scarborough all the time.'

CHAPTER 16

PAVILIONED IN SPLENDOUR

I

THERE ARE several ways of looking at the game of cricket; first, and probably best, it is a game played for enjoyment. It is an art, rich in the expression of subtle technical skills, where grace and strength may be magically blended. It is a vivid page in the history of its country, stretching from the enchanted ground of Broad Halfpenny Down to the grim battlefield of Bramall Lane and from the windy uplands of Lascelles Hall to the more majestic Members' and Friends' stand at Lord's. It is a long picaresque romance, as rich in comedy and character as *Don Quixote* or *Pickwick Papers*. It is also a fascinating form of controversy. It is spectacle, it is drama, it is good fun.

It is undoubtedly an art; an art that can give intense pleasure to those who practise it and to those who watch. The sight of a fibrositis-free Hutton driving a ball, like a streak of light, clear of mid-off or of Compton dancing out to sweep it away to leg with nonchalant precision : these are examples of high art and those who half a century ago looked on the wizardry of Trumper and Ranji carry with them the gleam and dazzle of it to this day. So do those who saw Frank Woolley stem the almost irresistible flood to score 95 and 93 against the Australians in the Lord's Test of 1921. There, if the watcher had an eye for any kind of beauty, was the perfection of lithe elegance and serene power. But the art of the great batsman is no mere nostalgic echo of the past, dreamed over by old gentlemen dozing in the sun. Go to the Oval and watch the living embodiment of a noble tradition, Peter May.

Cricket has written its name upon the scroll of English history. In the south it grew up as part and parcel of the green English countryside, and not only did it burgeon in

Hambledon; in Kent, in Surrey and in Sussex you would have found it, set against a lovely background of parkland or meadow.

Nor was it only in the gentler south that cricket came to life; it grew, too, in the rugged north, where life, or so they claimed, was more real, more earnest. A hundred years ago there battled its way into life the tradition of the game as it is played in the north: a hard, unrelenting tradition of imperturbable batting and Machiavellian bowling; a dour battle fought out before a critical cloth-capped audience that knew every twist and turn of the encounter. The crowd had its favourites and, lord, how it loved to chastise them . . . The same loving chastising spirit that moved the Sheffielders of the 'grinders' stand' to rag Tom Emmett without mercy still drives their descendants to reprove the peccant fieldsman: 'Bend thi' back!' or to adjure Yorkshire's former captain if by chance he fails to take a wicket: 'Bring on the twins!'

II

Cricket displays a mighty muster of character and characters, a bright pageant marching by from the good old days to the good new days. Cast an eye back to the Hambledon men: to Brett, of the 'tremendous bowling', to Tom Sueter, the first of the great wicket-keepers, of whom it was said that 'nothing went by him'; and to old Bob Robinson, who invented some queer batting pads of his own which covered his thighs with wood and his performance with ridicule from the 'fine brown-faced fellows of farmers' that formed the Hambledon crowd.

The pageant shoulders its way from the eighteenth into the nineteenth century. Here comes 'kind and manly' Alfred Mynn, who had hands like legs of mutton, weighed eighteen stone and could make the ball hum like a top when he bowled; and here is Fuller Pilch, the Norfolk man who settled in Canterbury to be a stalwart of Kent and an executant of forward play in all its grandeur; and here comes the schoolmaster-artist who preferred to be known as Felix, whose bat had the same grace and delicacy as his pencil, and who wrote a book, beautifully illustrated by himself, called *Felix on the*

Bat, which occasionally finds itself catalogued under the heading of Zoology.

And how solid and how brightly coloured were the characters who took the stage in the second half of the nineteenth century : the Doctor, the Champion, the great W.G., the Old Man himself, an Everest of a fellow, with his twinkling eye, his beard and his bulk and his surprisingly high-pitched voice squeaking : ' Well cot, well cot.' Or : ' May the best team win, and ain't we the best team?' Here is Tom (first-a-wide-and-then-a-wicket) Emmett, who took his first professional engagement at half-a-crown and walked to the game with the local newspaper as his cricket bag. Here is George (' Happy Jack ') Ulyett, who said that Yorkshire played him for his good behaviour and his whistling; and here Ephraim Lockwood, who could ' cut 'em straight off the middle ' and who, when called on to be impressed by the millions of gallons of water that went roaring over Niagara every hour, observed : ' I see nowt to stop it !' Here, too, are ' Tearaway ' Tarrant, the Tyson of the sixties, and John Jackson—' Jackson's pace is very fearful '—who never took all ten wickets but once took ' nine and lamed Johnny Wisden '; James Shaw, who twice bowled W.G. in his first over and twice saw him make over 200 in the second innings. (' I puts 'em where I likes and he puts 'em where *he* likes.') And there is Ted Pooley, the blithe cock-sparrow of a Surrey stumper whose fingers were gnarled like oak tree roots and to whom that iron fighter, the great Jem Mace, observed : ' Pooley, I'd rather stand in the ring for an hour than behind those stumps for five minutes.'

Recall the long sunlit cavalcade that graced the rich inter-war years : not merely the pre-eminent figures of the unquestionably great—Hobbs, Sutcliffe, the majestic Hammond and the incomparable Frank Woolley, but the chunky, loamy characters : Emmott Robinson (' It were wasted on thee ') or Cecil Parkin (' All right, Mr. Douglas, you bowl 'em in and I'll go on after tea and bowl 'em out ') or Arthur Wood, who once demanded of a batsman whose stumps had been grazed by three successive balls without shifting the bails : ' Have you ever tried walking on the water?' Or Maurice Leyland, chunkiest of them all, who wryly voiced for all time the feeling of the man in the middle : ' There you are and there's

thirty thousand people watching that know how to play the
bowling better than you do.' Or Patsy Hendren, the Cockney
darling of two hemispheres, who, when asked by an Australian
barracker if there existed anyone uglier than himself, replied
disarmingly : ' You should see my brother !'

It would be better to adopt a sceptical attitude towards
anyone who tells you that there are no real characters in
cricket today. Tell him to go and observe Johnny Wardle.
Johnny turns cricket into a glorious lark. Whether he is hitting sixes, or getting out, trying to hit sixes, or cajoling the
batsman into giving his wicket away, or ostentatiously stubbing his toe in imitation of that supremely individualistic
South African, ' Toey ' Tayfield, he can relax tension in the
atmosphere and keep spectators on good terms with themselves. If he tells a story it will be more often than not against
himself. He once had a leg-before-wicket decision turned
down—it would be a breach of security to say where—and
after the game was over he ventured mildly to ask the umpire : ' You know, I think that ball would have hit the wicket.
Where do you think it would have hit?' ' How should I
know?' replied the umpire with great show of reasonableness. ' The gentleman's leg was in the way.'

Have you noticed the amiably rustic expression with which
Gloucestershire's ' Bomber ' Wells sidles up to the wicket to
deliver a ball so innocent that the batsman hardly bothers to
play it and, as he pavilionwards plods his weary way, pensively wonders why he has been so foolish? Have you ever
studied the emotional reactions of Robin Marlar (a) when
he has just taken a wicket and (b) when he has just not taken
a wicket? It is, as they used to say when plays were good, as
good as a play.

And since we have introduced the subject of the drama,
have you ever watched, with a true dramatic critic's eye, the
matinée performances of Tony Lock in the field? At leg-slip
he will imitate the action of the tiger, stiffen the sinews,
summon up the blood and most certainly disguise fair nature
with hard-favoured rage. From the ringside I have never
been close enough to study the expression of his features, but
this is unnecessary. There is oratory in the set of his shoulders
and passion in the flapping of his shirt-sleeves; his appeal
for leg-before-wicket runs the gamut of all human emotions :

Insistence, Persuasion, Delight, or (if hard-heartedly refused) Incredulity and Despair. If a star pupil of the Royal Academy of Dramatic Art were to attempt to convey these varied degrees of human joy and suffering, he might find it difficult to express them all (to an audience behind his back) by eloquent movement of his dorsal muscles, but to Lock it presents no difficulties. (One almost wonders if this comes into the sphere of ballet as well as drama.) Besides all this, he is one of the best three close fieldsmen in England today (Stuart Surridge is the other two) and the most puzzling of all slow bowlers to England's visitors. In 1955, when the counties were running neck and neck, he had a batting average of 96 against Yorkshire. Let nobody assert the non-existence of delightful characters today.

III

Cricket is a lively argument. I remember recently talking to what is rather ironically called a sporting journalist. When I happened to say I disliked the hanging, drawing and quartering of the selection committee that was then being carried out in some newspapers, 'Ah,' said he, ' the public loves controversy.' That may be, yet I believe that the controversy cricket-lovers want is not the controversy which bandies smart-alec cracks, pries into the players' private lives and sets one decent fellow against another. Cricket's true controversy is the age-old noble controversy of bat and ball, between the art of the batsman and the fierceness or cunning of the bowler. These and these alone are ' the fell incensèd points of mighty opposites.'

Cricket is for the team and for the individual, and is one of the only institutions in the world that enables both team and individual to give of their best. The virtues of the team-game are sure as a rock : they need not be belauded or be-laboured. Cricket is an equally demanding (and rewarding) affair for the individual. Picture yourself sent out to defend your three straight sticks for half an hour in semi-darkness, with the fast bowler beginning his interminable run and three short-legs parked around your hip-pocket. Picture yourself, in short, being subjected to the full Newbolt treatment, breathless hush and all. A team-game? . . . Well, well . . .

Only the indomitable self-reliance of a Trevor Bailey will save you then.

Or imagine yourself standing, limbs a-tremble and nerves a-tingle, under a towering skier in the long field, while the insignificant but discreditable tale of your past life rolls before you like another bad film on the wide screen. You are alone in the universe, unless you are a person like Albert Knight, the old Leicestershire and England batsman, a Methodist local preacher and a man of shining integrity. Once he stood in the deep field while a near-six went rocketing above him. Would it fall behind him? He was right back on the rails. Suddenly the ball dipped and dropped like a stone. He fell forward on one knee. The crowd gasped and, as they saw the ball at last come to rest cleanly in Knight's cupped hands, broke into a cheer. For a moment he remained quite still, head bent.

' Hullo, Albert,' called his captain. ' What are you up to there?'

' Sir,' he replied simply, ' I was thanking my Maker.'

But, setting aside the possibility of divine intervention, in which Albert Knight believed with spotless sincerity, you must reckon that, humanly speaking, you are alone. Nobody can help you : not the captain, not the committee, not the Welfare State. This is your battle and you must fight it. Cricket has been a prime encourager of such a fighter.

Cricket is entertainment. High entertainment in all its rainbow riches came to us from Compton and Edrich in 1947, from the dashing Neil Harvey in 1953, and from Roy McLean, whose batting had the colour of a field of May-flowering tulips, in 1955. Sometimes the critics rage furiously in their demand that entertainment should come first all the time, but I am not certain if they know what they mean by entertainment.

The word is not wholly circumscribed by the hitting of sixes, satisfying though that form of violence may be. Entertainment may lie in an infinite variety of good things : in quick running between the wickets (where the run-stealers flicker to and fro); in the skilful ' farming ' of the bowling that keeps the wolf from the weaker batsman's door; in the keen-edged battle of wits between the batsman who will *not* be cabined and confined, and the bowler who refuses to be hit off his length; and, above all (as I think), in sure, clean and meticulously accurate ground fielding.

I would rather leave the question of entertainment to the cricketers themselves, because I believe that entertainment rises naturally to its highest form when the players are playing to the best of their own individual abilities and skills, in the game's every phase, for the game's own primary purpose.

Cricket has an element of poetry. I was recently sitting on a club settee wtih an acquaintance, talking of this and that, when suddenly, without warning, he exclaimed: 'A. C. Mac-Laren and C. B. Fry.'

'True,' said I, 'and Johnny Tyldesley and Ranji.'

'F. S. Jackson and Braund.'

'G. L. Jessop and George Hirst.'

'Lilley, Lockwood and Wilfred Rhodes.'

'The English team in the Birmingham Test of 1902,' I agreed, 'and reckoned the best eleven ever put into the field anywhere.'

'It's more than that,' cried my friend. 'The very names are pure poetry.'

Foolish? Foolish indeed, but the other fellow was one of the greatest of living writers, whose name I will not disclose, lest I should be accused of snobbery in claiming his acquaintance.

I will end as I began, with the fine hymn line, '*Pavilioned in Splendour*,' to which I would listen in church, and think, with true reverence, of Lord Hawke, until I was bemused and enchanted by the glory of two words. Pavilion . . . Splendour . . . There was something in these two words that placed the game on the level of the Round Table, surrounded by noble knights, gentle but incredibly brave. So cricketers, seen through the eyes of a child, seemed heroes, paladins . . . And, after half a disillusioning century, cricketers have been far less disillusioning than other paladins.

Cricket in a most unassuming way is a form of civilisation; its courtesies comprise true civility in the sense in which Sir Harold Nicholson has employed the word: 'I believe that civility, however it may alter its shape and colouring, is based upon reason and affection which, in spite of recent evidence, are eternal.' Another poet has spoken of the game with the same reasonableness and affection:

Patient, dramatic, serious, genial,
From over to over the game goes on,
Weaving a pattern of hardy perennial
Civilisation under the sun.

And cricket, last as well as first, free from all sententious-
ness, is a pleasant game for a summer day between people
who can respect each other on the field and like each other off
it. Those who love it best will strive to keep it so.

EPILOGUE:

'TO THE ONE I LOVED THE BEST'

O N 10TH May, 1954, died George Herbert Hirst, great all-round cricketer and great gentleman. It was always agreed that the greatest all-rounder in the game's history came from the little stone-built village of Kirkheaton, but it was never completely agreed what his name was. Many people have said it was George Hirst. Hirst himself always said it was Wilfred Rhodes. For over half a century these two were comrades, friends and neighbours. When they were playing for Yorkshire or England, there never was a more formidable pair.

A few years older than Rhodes, Hirst played for his village at fourteen, and had a county trial at eighteen. Three years later he became a regular member of the side and in 1893 he helped Yorkshire to win the first of their many championships. That was the year in which he made 35 not out against Gloucestershire, a brave total in a low-scoring match which made W.G. say: 'I never knew the beggar could bat as well . . .'

Year after year he went on being the heart and soul of a conquering eleven. With Rhodes, Haigh and Jackson, he was the spearhead of a damaging attack and, even in a side sustained and coloured by Tunnicliffe, Brown and Denton, he was the county's most dangerous bat. He was a match-winner in the sense that only Keith Miller of the present day has been a match-winner: one whose batting or bowling might at any moment change the whole issue of a game.

He retired from the Yorkshire side in 1921, though he turned out at least once as late as 1929, somewhere around his fifty-eighth birthday. For nearly the whole of the time between the wars he was coach at Eton, and a splendid coach he was: shrewd, wise, imaginative and infinitely kindly. He was custodian, too, of the Headingley nets, those portals that opened a glittering future to the talented and fortunate few. At Headingley many are called and few are chosen, but in Hirst's time there was never a lad who was not helped and encouraged to the limit of his power and skill.

Hirst's records are in the book and could make a record book of themselves. In all he scored over 36,000 runs, took over 2,700 wickets, and made 518 catches. As for the all-rounder's double, only his friend Rhodes, with sixteen times, surpassed him. Hirst scored a thousand runs and took a hundred wickets fourteen times; three of these times included 2,000 runs and one of them, 1906, Hirst's year of wonders, saw him credit himself with 2,385 runs and 208 wickets. No one has ever approached this fantastic feat since, and I do not believe anyone ever will. In 1901, his first year of greatness, he made 1,950 runs and took 183 wickets, and from 1903 to 1913 he never missed a ' double.'

He played in twenty-four Tests. Some say that he gave his best for Yorkshire, rather than for England. Unquestionably he gave of his superlative best for Yorkshire, but it is as certain that he never let England down. In the first Test of 1902 he and Rhodes flung the Australians out for 36 on a reasonably good pitch, and, although Rhodes got seven of the wickets, it was Hirst who ' rattled ' them first. (In the Australians' very next match, against Yorkshire at Leeds, they were dismissed by Hirst and Jackson for 23, Hirst five for 9.) In the ever memorable Jessop's Test of the same year, Hirst was the second hero, with 58 not out, and as we have noted earlier, it was no disrespect to Jessop's dazzling exploit to say that if George Hirst, with help from Lockwood, had not stubbornly saved the follow-on in the first innings, the match might never have brought its added immortality to Jessop's name. It is also a fact that in the first Test of Warner's 1903-04 Australian tour, Hirst's fearless 60 not out at a critical period saved a match which might have been lost, had he faltered.

He began as a straight fast bowler and only developed his slightly diabolical ' swerve ' round about the turn of the century. On his swerving day hardly anyone could play him. His swerver must have been a fearsome ball to deal with; its victims said it came suddenly at you like a fierce throw-in from cover. His batting was not elegant; like himself, it was honest, open-hearted and lusty. He gloried in a tremendous pull-stroke and, when he played it, fieldsmen scattered like leaves before Shelley's wild west wind. He made 56 centuries, including a 300 and more than one 200, but some of his best innings were smaller scores, put together in the task of getting Yorkshire or England out of trouble. He was the best mid-off I ever saw and only A. E. R. Gilligan was anything like as good. Nearly all his 518 catches were rasping ones, for a full-blooded drive seldom comes at you gently. The ball went into his hands, in Tom Emmett's phrase, ' as safe as an old coal-box.' He enjoyed fielding, as he enjoyed batting and bowling, for the sheer zest of the thing. At Lord's or the Oval, at Sydney or Melbourne, he was greeted by a multitude of friends. In Yorkshire he was beloved; over a long period he *was* Yorkshire.

Beyond all his prowess as a player and his skill as a coach, there was something more : a something that lay in his generous soul and indomitable spirit. He was a sturdy man, physically and morally. As a person he was so deep-rooted in his honesty that he was incapable of a mean action, on or off the field. His virtue was not self-conscious. His humour and humanity were so mixed in him, his qualities were so finely balanced that he might have stood for the ideal York-shireman, even the ideal Englishman, a citizen of that half-mythical, half-mystical England,

Where the primroses bloom and the nightingales sing
And the honest poor man is as good as a king.

George was indeed a king and a more gracious monarch never held court in England's green and pleasant land.

He had all Yorkshire's strength and more than Yorkshire's grace. He was forthright, even blunt, but his bluntness was softened by old-fashioned courtesy. When he bowled against you, he did not ' hate ' you, as some famous bowlers are reputed to have done; he merely did you the honour of giving you the best that was in him; and in that generous spirit he sent your middle stump cartwheeling. He would not have known the meaning of ' defensive ' bowling. He meant to get a wicket with every ball he bowled. When he held a bat, every stroke he made with it was intended as an active contribution towards victory. The daughter who was the loved and loving companion of his last years wrote to me : ' I shall miss him very much. We have always been such good friends, but he has had a long life and a good life and I suppose no one could ask for more.'

There were great cricketers before; there are great cricketers now, and, happily, there will be great cricketers again. But in the history of the game George Hirst will always hold his own shining place. A noble game is the nobler because he played it and to every lad he taught, to every man who knew him, he will ever remain the gentle master and the living inspiration.

INDEX

THE PAVILION LIBRARY

New Titles

Australia 63
Alan Ross

Pavilioned in Splendour
A. A. Thomson

Backlist

Cricket Cauldron
Alex Bannister

Double Century Vol I
Marcus Williams (ed.)

Masters of Cricket
Jack Fingleton

Double Century Vol II
Marcus Williams (ed.)

Cricket All His Life
E. V. Lucas

In Search of Cricket
J. M. Kilburn

The Cricket Captains of England
Alan Gibson

Sort of a Cricket Person
E. W. Swanton

Farewell to Cricket
Don Bradman

End of an Innings
Denis Compton

Jack Hobbs
Ronald Mason

Ranji
Alan Ross

In Celebration of Cricket
Kenneth Gregory

Batter's Castle
Ian Peebles

The Best Loved Game
Geoffrey Moorhouse

The Ashes Crown the Year
Jack Fingleton

Bowler's Turn
Ian Peebles

Life Worth Living
C. B. Fry

Lord's 1787-1945
Sir Pelham Warner

Cricket Crisis
Jack Fingleton

Lord's 1946-1970
Diana Rait Kerr and Ian Peebles

P. G. H. Fender
Richard Streeton

Through the Caribbean
Alan Ross

Hirst and Rhodes
A. A. Thomson